Ov

From Australia

Ewen Levick

A book for those who helped me on the way.

Note: Some names have been changed and others edited.

While every precaution has been taken in the preparation of this book, the author assumes no responsibility for errors or omissions, or for damages resulting from the use of the information contained herein.

Overland
Copyright © 2019 Ewen Levick.

ISBN: 978-0-646-80520-7

TABLE OF CONTENTS

The Desert | 4
The Sea | 19
The Islands | 37
The Lake | 57
The Plain | 77
The Jungle | 97
The Cities | 110
The Steppe | 136
The Road | 151
The Forest | 168
The Mountains | 185
The Valleys | 207
The Meadows | 228
The End | 241
Epilogue

1
THE DESERT

The village of Pearl Springs, China, stretches along the floor of a deep, forested valley. It is a small place, shaded by the surrounding mountains, that can be found at the end of a narrow road winding through well-kept groves of green trees. The few inhabitants live on both sides of a small, clear brook babbling its merry way through their quiet village. It is a place far from the currents, and this suits the people of Pearl Springs just fine. They are happy to grow walnuts and chestnuts in their tended groves and send them on to markets in bigger places, just as they have done for a long, long time.

If you stand in the centre of Pearl Springs, in a concrete courtyard outside the primary school, you can just make out a thin grey line stretching across the jagged mountain ridge high above. That thin grey line, unclear from this distance, stretches across 21,000 kilometres of northern Asia. It is the Great Wall of China.

If you, overtaken by curiosity and a sudden sense of adventure, decide to have a closer look at the Wall, simply walk to the far end of the village and you will find a small access road leading upwards into the forest. It follows the brook for a time, which shrinks as the land rises until the waters are no more than a rivulet struggling through leaves on the forest floor.

The road, you'll find, is now a dirt path that leaves the brook and begins to wind its way steadily up the steepening hillside. It is heavy going now, more of a climb than a walk. The trees cling to the ground with knobbled roots and rustle gently in greeting when you trudge past.

Eventually the trees give way and reveal the Wall. It is

an imposing face of grey rock that stares at you impassively, confident in its own might but crumbling with age. There is a staircase leading to the top.

If you climb the stairs and continue to follow the Wall as it leads up the ridge, you will soon arrive at an isolated watchtower sitting atop the highest peak around. The views are now vast and your gaze drifts across the serrated green mountain ridges into a blue distance that becomes sky only when the Earth itself curves away. Pearl Springs sits at your feet - now just a strip of red roofs and cleared fields dwarfed by the planetary scale of the surrounding mountains. It is enough to make you pause. The wind is cold and strong here and pulls your hair back from your face.

The watchtower itself, however, is dark and has a foreboding air. It is almost like you are walking into someone else's house uninvited. There is an eerie sense that they are silently watching your approach.

Curiosity, though, is a powerful thing. Whoever built this place is surely long gone - only a crumbling remnant has been left behind. It is also cold on the open Wall and you are too exposed to that mighty roar of wind flying up the mountainside. The watchtower offers shelter.

If curiosity and the strong wind at your back did indeed push you into the dark watchtower and did so on one particularly chilly May evening, you would've found a man with an unkempt ginger beard wearing nothing but shorts, a thin green raincoat and socks stuck to his feet by dried blood and broken blisters, shivering and tilting his head back as he desperately shakes the last drops of honey out of a small glass jar into his chattering mouth.

This is a story of the series of questionable decisions that lead that man to be in that watchtower on that chilly May evening. That man, if you haven't already guessed, is me.

—

A quick Google search has just told me that it is 16,623 kilometres from Sydney, Australia to Basel, Switzerland, in a straight line. The door-to-door travel time is roughly 32 hours via Dubai and London. This is a trip I've made a few times - my parents live in Basel and I live in Sydney. I'm not sure when the idea of travelling to Switzerland without flying first occurred to me, but it was a few years before finally having the time and money to do so.

I first revealed the idea to my girlfriend, Danika, who managed to hide her concerns about my safety well enough to outwardly support the plan. The next person to know was my friend Omair. I told him over dinner about three months before I was free to leave.

"So when are you flying to Switzerland?" he asked while we both sawed into slightly overdone steaks.

"Actually," I replied. "I'm thinking I'll try and make my way back without flying."

He chuckled and continued sawing. The conversation drifted elsewhere, then after a pause he asked again.

"But seriously. When are you flying back?"

"Seriously, I'm not," I said again. "I'm going to try and go overland."

The sawing stopped. He looked at me intently. "You can't be serious."

"I really am," I insisted. "I can find a boat to Singapore and go from there."

"Dude," he said, slowly lowering his knife and fork. "What? How?"

I shrugged. "Well I'm sure you can go from Singapore

to Beijing without flying and you can definitely take the Trans-Siberian from Beijing to Moscow. It makes sense on paper."

He wasn't convinced and to be honest, I wasn't either. I decided to just travel as far in the direction of Switzerland as possible and enjoy the journey while it lasted.

Having saved the money, found the time and made the decision, I started researching crew positions on small yachts sailing to the Asian mainland, or at least to Indonesia. Unfortunately, none were heading that far north. People preferred to sail to less pirate-y places like New Zealand and Tasmania. It began to seem like I'd fallen at the first hurdle.

After two months of fruitless searching I eventually found a cruise ship that was leaving Perth in two months, heading to Singapore. After mulling it over for a few weeks I called the company number on an impulse as I disembarked a ferry in Sydney. It was just before the Christmas holidays and the Australian summer sun was beating down. I sat on a nearby bench overlooking the harbour just as a woman answered the phone with an enthusiastic voice.

"Hello and thanks for calling Princess Cruises, my name is Christine, how can I help you today?"

I introduced myself and explained my fledgling plan. "I'm on a very tight budget, so is there any way to get a reduced price? Can I leave the cruise early or share a room with another solo traveller?"

"Unfortunately not," Christine replied. "You can leave early but that will have to be arranged with the captain and you will still have to pay the full price."

I sighed. "What about sharing a room?"

"We don't arrange that kind of thing," she said. "But…" - I heard some tapping in the background – "there are websites where you can try and find someone that will split the cost of a room with you."

"And when is the latest that I should buy a ticket?"

More tapping. "Well, it's filling up fast, although you might be able to get last minute tickets if there are cancellations. If you find someone we can arrange for them to come on-board but they will have to pay their share to you directly."

I thought for a moment. The ferry pulled away from the dock with a low rumble, churning the sunlit water into rolls of sparkling white foam. A cruise wasn't the rugged and adventurous beginning to the trip that I'd envisaged. It would also eat a huge chunk of my budget. Yet the urge to make a decision suddenly gripped me.

"Yes," I heard myself saying. "I'll get a ticket."

"You will?" Christine asked, audibly surprised.

"Yeah. Charge me before I change my mind."

And so, the stage was set. I travelled to Melbourne by car and by bus to spend the last few weeks in Australia with Danika and her family. Danika was due to fly to Basel in four months' time, roughly 130 days. This gave me a time frame to work with and more importantly, a source of motivation for the road.

I began looking at route options while I was in Melbourne. Unfortunately, the most direct route, south of the Caspian Sea – through India, Pakistan, Iran, Turkey and Greece – would take me through too many war zones. Afghanistan was also a major obstacle, as was Tibet and the Indian border with Myanmar, which is closed to foreigners. The only roads passed through China.

The most viable option, I decided, was to travel north. I would head to China and to Siberia, and then head west. This had the added benefit of taking me through Mongolia, a country that had captured my imagination ever since I watched Ewan

McGregor and Charley Boorman cross it in their documentary series, Long Way Round, when I was a kid. I now had passage to Asia, a pot of money and a workable plan.

—

Soon enough the time came to leave. I repacked my bag, double-checking that I had everything I thought I needed and trying to imagine things I needed but hadn't yet thought of. How many shorts should I take? Do I need to buy more razors? What if I can't get a Russian visa? Is this all too crazy? Should I bring this big deodorant can or stick with the little one that's in my pack?

Danika drove me to Melbourne's Southern Cross Station, where I was due to catch a train towards Adelaide. It sat waiting for the whistle to pull away. Suddenly every second we had left together was immeasurably valuable. Danika was crying (although this isn't unusual) and I took some deep breaths, doing my best to savour the last moments and at the same time wondering whether it was too late to back out.

In the end the train guard made the decision for me. He blew his whistle and I rushed on-board just when the train began to pull away. Danika soon disappeared from view, replaced by a sudden flash of bright morning sunshine. It had begun.

The city shrunk away as we crawled through Melbourne's suburbs before these too shrunk away into a flat yellow landscape. One by one most other passengers fell asleep. I stared out the window, dwelling on the fact that I'd just caught a train to Switzerland and watching the golden hills rise and fall.

I disembarked in Bendigo, got on the bus to Adelaide and resumed staring. The landscape remained unchanged over the day - nine slow hours passing through nothing but flat yellow farmland and dilapidated towns that seemed to be under some collective illusion that they weren't located in a dusty nowhere.

We passed through one place where council workers were mowing the dirt on the side of the road, watched by a shirtless dude absentmindedly fiddling with his left nipple. A few minutes later I saw another man raking the dirt in his front garden as if it was a lush and green lawn.

The passing views became hypnotically surreal, nothing but a wheaty expanse dotted with rusting last-century tractors and rickety iron windmills. The power lines outside the window rose up and down, up, down, lifting and lowering my eyelids in unison. Most passengers fell asleep. Their heads flopped spinelessly from side to side. I made my first journal entry – "a good thing power-lines don't kill birds" – and promptly joined in.

—

The bus pulled into Adelaide in the early evening, just as the streetlights were flickering on. I hoisted my pack and set off to find a McDonalds to charge my phone and get something to eat.

After a bit of a wander I found one near North Terrace, Adelaide's main street and used to opportunity to look for accommodation. It was late and few places had any room and those that did were expensive. Oh well, I thought. Adelaide is entirely surrounded by parkland. I can probably just find somewhere and lie down for free.

I walked through the train station and over the river towards a deserted football stadium, where I found an inviting fig tree with enormous roots rising like walls half a metre out of the ground. I rolled my sleeping bag out in-between the roots, screened from both sides and settled in.

I slept well enough at first, but was woken at around two in the morning by a crippling stomach cramp. I let it pass and drifted back off.

Another one followed and woke me up again. Each cramp was more painful than the last. I felt like I was going into labour.

After two or so hours of trying to snatch sleep between contractions, I decided enough was enough and set off to find a toilet. I stumbled back across the river towards the train station. Movement made everything worse. I doubled over in pain and desperately sucked at the air. I had a pressure cooker in my abdomen that was about to explode and spray chunks of Ewen everywhere.

I reached the train station toilets and spent twenty minutes sitting with my head in my hands. It was four in the morning. What series of terrible decisions had led me here? Last night I was in a comfortable and warm bed in Melbourne, looking forward to a hot breakfast and coffee and now I was alone, in Adelaide, waiting for the sunrise on a cold steel toilet.

I walked around awhile and watched the city slowly wake up. Street sweepers with flashing orange lights hummed past and the clunk of coffee shop tables being set out on the pavement echoed down empty streets. I found an open café and settled down with a local paper. Unsurprisingly there wasn't much happening in Adelaide, but then again, I'm not sure if much ever does.

I was soon due to catch the train to Perth, the Indian Pacific, so I caught a tram to the southern edge of the business district, hoisted my pack and plunged into yet another park. Plodding on through the relentless heat, I eventually broke out of the bush, dishevelled and dehydrated, and into a district of low office blocks and railway lines. The station was at the end of an obscure driveway.

I checked in my luggage and boarded the train, where I discovered that I'd spend the next two days living with less legroom than a broom cupboard. The seat reclined by the tiniest fraction (if you stretch the definition of 'recline' to its absolute limit). I thought a $350 ticket would at least win me a flat surface to sleep on, but it bought passage to Perth on a chair and only that; no food, no pillow, no blankets. One shower was shared between at least thirty people.

I found a seat, dropped my bag in the seat next to me and stared out the window.

A stench suddenly permeated the carriage. It was followed soon after by an enormous mumbling man. He was hugely overweight, dressed in loose tracksuits with sandals on - the sort of person that makes you realise your life isn't going so badly after all, even if you did just spend a significant part of your morning sitting on a cold steel toilet.

Everyone eyed him warily. He shuffled slowly down the aisle. The other passengers coughed and retched. Each empty seat he passed crushed my hopes a little further. He kept shuffling slowly forward, then stopped at my row. Dear God, no. It's always me.

"Forty-two, hruthth frethth", he mumbled as he dropped his considerable bulk into the chair, causing the entire carriage to sway from side to side. A smell crawled down my throat.

"I'm Harris, ra mruthth," he said, sticking out a meaty hand.

"Ewen," I gasped. His hand felt like ham left out in the sun.

"Looks like this is us for two days", Harris observed, croaking out the last syllable for a second too long. "Tthth. Not a lot of room." His hairy torso spilt out of his shirt and over the armrest into my seat.

A greying man in a fluorescent vest strode in and stood at the front of the carriage. He wrinkled his nose and gave us a look of absolute disdain.

"If I catch any of you smoking in here, I'll kick you off at the next stop. Absolutely nobody is to enter the restaurant car without shoes. If I catch you in there without shoes I'll kick you off at the next stop. You are to remain in this carriage and the restaurant car. If I catch you in any other carriage I'll kick you off at the next stop." He turned on his heel and marching out the way he came.

Harris shifted his bulk and let out a sigh. "Withth shthth mmmm."

—

After another uncomfortable night, I woke suddenly and coughed out the thick stench that had settled in my lungs. Harris was snoring away next to me.

I rubbed my eyes and rolled up the blinds. A dim orange glow was just visible on the horizon as the train slid slowly past small, gnarled trees. I saw an opportunity and snuck into the Gold Class carriage for a decent shower before the staff started prowling around.

Over the morning the trees grew steadily smaller. Around lunchtime they stopped altogether, replaced by a flat expanse of ankle-high scrub and football-sized rocks stretching to a distant, shimmering horizon. We had entered the Nullarbor.

A Latin phrase (null arbor) meaning no trees, the Nullarbor is a vast and unforgiving wilderness that provides me with plenty of mind-boggling facts to share with you. Daytime temperatures regularly hit 50 degrees Celsius in summer, while on winter nights it drops to -7. The immense Martian landscape stretches 1100 kilometres from east to west and contains the world's longest straight section of railway - 478 kilometres, which is the distance between London and the Scottish border. The entire plain is almost the size of Belarus. To the north of the

Nullarbor is the Great Victoria Desert, which is only slightly smaller than Germany; beyond that is the Gibson Desert, the size of Nepal; and even further north is the Great Sandy Desert, roughly the size of Ecuador. To the south lies nothing but ocean until Antarctica. It is the end of the earth.

To add to the extra-terrestrial feel of the Nullarbor, it was also impossible to know the time. Western Australia is two and a half hours behind Adelaide, but I didn't have a watch and my phone resolutely refused to leave Adelaide time. The view outside was entirely featureless. I found myself adrift on an unchanging and utterly inhospitable landscape with no idea where I was, how fast I was moving, or the time of day.

I settled myself in the restaurant car, which was outfitted like a 1950s American diner, to read my book or look out the window in a hypnotic trance. Scrub and rock slid endlessly past my eyes for hours and unmoving white clouds grew smaller over the distance before the sky curved sharply down into a horizon made wobbly and indeterminate by sparkling mirages. The tracks were dead straight, keeping the rest of the train out of sight. The regular rumbling of the wheels was interrupted only by the occasional announcement of something menial and unnecessary over the deafening PA system.

Other passengers began drifting into the diner. Harris's fumes entered, followed shortly thereafter by Harris. He started scribbling strange signs in a small notebook and mumbling quietly.

A megaphone above our heads crackled to life. "I JUST NEED TO TEST THE PA SYSTEM," a woman bellowed.

The silence returned, but only for a moment.

"JUST A TEST, I'M NOW TESTING," the woman screamed. "I REPEAT: TESTING, TESTING."

I closed my eyes and listened to Harris scribble with renewed vigour.

After sunset, we pulled into a cluster of buildings that advertised itself as Forrest - population 18. The passengers in Gold Class enjoyed a tabletop dinner outside, serenaded by a guy with a guitar, while those of us in backpacker class huddled around a bin fire in the cold dark. Our angry carriage attendant strode back and forth, fixing us with watchful eyes. Harris stood alone and smoked furiously.

At one point a few brave Chinese backpackers wandered towards the tantalising smell of food. The carriage attendant bellowed and sprinted after them, beat them unconscious with his fists and drag their flaccid bodies back to our pitiful circle.

—

The next morning revealed a familiar landscape of rolling brown hills. This, to cut a long story short, continued all day. I had to sit through that in mind-numbing boredom, but this is a book, so I'll do you a favour and just gloss right over it.

In the late afternoon the Indian Pacific finally ended its transcontinental journey by coming to a gradual, wheezing stop at East Perth Terminal.

The megaphone squealed painfully. "YOU MIGHT HAVE NOTICED WE'VE ARRIVED IN PERTH," the woman roared. "JUST TO REPEAT, THIS IS PERTH AND WE'VE NOW ARRIVED."

"Best of luck with your travels, mmmff", mumbled Harris.

"ALL STAFF YOU CAN UNLOCK YOUR DOORS. THE TRAIN HAS ARRIVED IN PERTH."

"Thanks, Harris," I replied, shaking his sweaty hand.

I left the confines of the train into the bright afternoon

sunlight and made my way down to a crowd of people waiting for luggage. A man with a grey beard fell into step next to me.

"Have you got somewhere to stay?" he asked while we walked along the platform. He had what sounded like a strong American accent.

"Not yet," I responded. "I figured I'd find somewhere now."

"Well I'm staying at the YHA, ey," he said, "28 dollars a night. I always stay at YHAs and they're great. I can show you where it is if you're interested."

"Yeah, sure. How far is it?"

"Oh, just a block or two that way, ey." He indicated somewhere to our left.

He'd mentioned his name but I'd already forgotten it. I'm like that with names – I forget them just moments after someone has introduced themselves. I'd have to wait until he revealed it again. In the meantime, he would be known as 'Man'.

"Sorry Man, ready to go. Where did you say it was?"

"Oh, not far," Man said with a syrupy 'r'. "Not far at all, ey."

We later set off for a drink in a two-storey pub with a wraparound bull-nose veranda. Man ordered two beers at the bar, bonded briefly with the Canadian bartender and insisted on paying.

"No, no, I can pay," I protested.

"Nonsense," Man said. "I was a student once and I know what it's like. People bought me drinks when I was young and now it's my turn to pay it forward, ey."

We found a table on the terrace and passed an hour or two talking away, mostly about hunting and oil. His name, as it eventually turned out, was Dave. Dave was Canadian and loved to travel around Australia. When he wasn't doing this, he lived on a large farm just short of the Arctic Circle, where he spent the majority of his time shooting moose and collecting antique guns. He had three granddaughters who also enjoyed shooting moose. As I've never shot a moose I can't say we had a whole lot in common, but it was good to have company.

I suggested dinner, so we wandered down the street and found a place that sold emu, camel, kangaroo and crocodile steaks. I ordered the emu. It tasted like stringy beef. Dave paid again. I pushed money towards him but he was having none of it.

"That's for putting up with an old man for a few hours," he said. "It's been a pleasure. If you're ever in Canada, let me know, ey. I'll show you how to shoot some moose. Ey!"

—

The morning of the cruise arrived. I packed my bag excitedly, left my expensive fast-drying travel towel hanging on the back of the shower door and set off for Fremantle, a suburb of Perth fronting the Indian Ocean.

As the train pulled into the station the ship came into view. It was simply massive, easily the size of an office building or a city hotel. Strings of flags stretched along its length like bunting fluttering gently in the breeze and the sun shone off its gleaming white hull.

I'd reached the moment of departure from Australian shores. I made a last-minute phone call before cancelling my mobile account, then checked in to the cruise and filed through customs. I then climbed some stairs, opened a door into a waiting area and came face to face with an enormous herd of old people.

There were thousands of them, a crowd of shrink-wrapped skeletons occupying every seat in the building. They all turned and stared at me with decaying, yellow eyeballs sunken back into wrinkled skulls. Some looked like they'd actually just sat down and died. Those that seemed more alive sat and dribbled furiously.

I knew that the cruise was likely to have a lot of elderly aboard - the ship could hold 2500 passengers - but it seemed as if there were 2499 people on the brink of death and me. I took a breath in, held and released. The air was musty.

After a long wait we boarded the ship in a long and senile line. I dropped my pack in my room and moved to what I think was the poop deck to await the moment we'd set sail. Three long, low notes blared from the ship's horn when the engines fired. A tumult of water rumbled up. We slid away from the dock, then out of the small harbour.

I stood still and stared out with my hands on the rail. The sun was setting red over the water, throwing golden shafts of light through the isolated sheets of rain chasing the ship. I'd found it difficult to enjoy myself without Danika and wished she was here. Everything seemed harder to appreciate alone.

The shore sailed further and further away, then vanished.

2
THE SEA

I am named after my grandfather. Other than my name, he also gave me a red beard and hairy legs. Lastly, he gave me his ring: a simple square of green stone flecked with red. I gave the ring to my mum for safekeeping before I left. So, in a sense, this journey I was undertaking wasn't dissimilar Frodo's in The Lord of the Rings, except he battled through the dangers of Middle Earth to throw his in a fiery volcano and defeat evil, whereas I cruised in luxury through the Indian Ocean with a load of crusty old people to put mine back on my left pinkie finger.

Many thoughts like these wandered through my mind during the three-day trip from Fremantle to Indonesia. There were a number of activities on board, but these were mostly freemason meet-ups, chocolate spa treatments, back pain relief, or lessons in acupuncture and fat loss (Lose Six Inches Now!). One particularly popular activity seemed to be stopping in the hallways and staring brainlessly at the wall. The ship was filled with chairs and covered in signs warning me not to trip on stairs, scald myself in the shower, get blown over on the deck, or block the hallways with my wheelchair. Old age began to feel contagious.

The ship itself though was a thing of absolute luxury. It had a four-story atrium with two glass-encased lifts, a fountain and palm trees stretching almost to the third floor. Elsewhere there was a basketball court, three small swimming pools, a number of hot tubs, a spa, a hairdresser, twelve elevators, a gym, three restaurants, three dining halls, a café, a library, two theatres, a nightclub, a pub, a burger grill, three bars and a number of shops selling jewellery and travel essentials. The open deck even had an enormous movie screen overlooking the swimming pools.

And the best part: almost all the food was free. I could order as many pizzas as I could eat at the pizzeria, unlimited ham and cheese croissants or chocolate mousse at the café, or endless handmade omelettes in the dining hall. I can shamelessly say that I gorged. I would pile breakfast plates full of diabetes and eat a toasted sandwich two hours later. In fact, every time the thought of food even flickered through my dozing mind I waddled down to the café and ate a croissant. The cooks at the pizzeria even started using me as a guinea pig for experimental pizzas. I was fattening myself up for the lean times ahead and I loved every minute.

I settled in for a relaxed journey north. I paced in big circles around the deck, listening to podcasts and radio comedy. Occasionally I ventured inside for food or lounged on a deck chair. The ocean stretched to an unbroken horizon in every direction, the deep blue broken only by white caps and a tumble of white water pushing away from the ship's bow. A sky-blue scar of bubbles on the water's surface was the only sign of our passing.

The ship slid forward and the ocean backward. My vision swirled. Other passengers walking the deck moved in slow zigzags according to the gentle roll of the waves. All the while the sun beat relentlessly down on this floating, palatial care home.

During one of these walks something flickered in the corner of my vision: a bird swooping low and fast above the surface of the water. I turned, confused by the presence of a bird so far from shore, but it was gone. I dismissed it as another illusion and continued my walk.

A ship passed in the far distance, its silhouette only just

visible against a hazy white horizon, before slipping out of sight. The view returned to an endless expanse of restless blue.

Then, all of a sudden, wings flickered again. I hauled my body out of the deck chair I'd settled in and peered over the railing. There was nothing but the rhythmic white wash rolling away from the ship's side.

Suddenly a fish leapt out of the water, spread its wings and flew thirty metres before plopping back into the water with a splash. I blinked, rubbed my eyes and kept watching. A few minutes later another one popped out, then two at the same time. An older couple walked past and I beckoned them over.

I hadn't spoken all day, so my voice came out like gravel crunching under car tires. "Have you guys seen the flying fish?"

"No! Are there some here?" the woman asked. They peered over the rail.

"Well I just saw a few," I said. "Although now that I've called you over there won't be any more."

"That'd be Murphy's law," the man laughed.

"They were leaping out of the water here and flying a good distance."

We watched the water, but nothing happened. Just when I was about to break the silence, three fish leapt out of the wake and flew for almost ten seconds.

"There's some!" the woman exclaimed. "Did you see those, Terry?"

"Sure did," the man responded. "Funny little things aren't they."

The fish continued to leap out of the water, their scales glinting in the sun to glide above the waves. We stood and conversed while watching the fish. Their names were Terry and Kim from Perth and this was their first ocean cruise. They complained about the long lines of fat people queuing for food. I laughed in agreement. It was nice to make some friends, adrift as I was amongst the nearly dead.

Each day passed the same way. I ate food, lay on deck chairs, occasionally checked to see if the people next to me were still breathing and tried to take photos of fish.

On the morning of the third day, I woke up, showered and went out on deck to have a look around. The heat settled over me like a blanket and sweat beaded on my forehead. A hazy white mist shrouded the horizon. The ocean was still, as still as I had seen it and the ship slid softly over the top like it was floating just above the surface, the background to someone's dream. We were approaching the tropics.

—

A door slammed in the hallway. My cabin was black as pitch. Groggy and disorientated, I patted the bedside table in search of my phone, checked the time and then rolled out of bed. Somewhere on the other side of this black void was a light switch. I struck out into the darkness and immediately crunched my toes into a chair.

I got dressed and went out on deck to see where we were. Other ships were scattered in the water around us. A rusty barge sat a few hundred metres away, set amongst a scattering of colourful wooden fishing boats with high prows covered in lines of slack rope. The humidity was thick, the sun hidden behind a thin film of hazy cloud. The ship had anchored a kilometre or two off Bali. It was almost a surprise to see other humans.

We boarded a ferry to the port and were quickly met by a throng of Balinese taxi men offering rides around the island. They flocked around me like moths to a candle.

"Hi sir, where are you going?"

"No, thanks, I'm just walking," I replied.

"Yes, yes, where are you going?" they said in unison. I pushed further through the growing crowd. Some were almost frothing at the mouth.

An older guy approached. "Hello, yes, where are you going?" he asked.

I looked at him and realised I actually had no idea.

"I don't actually know," I said. "I was hoping to get to a temple or something."

"Yes, temple, yes, I take you there all day for seventy Australian dollar," he said excitedly.

I raised my eyebrows and let out a breath of air. "Seventy! That's way too much for me."

"Ok, ok, fifty," he said.

"I wasn't going to spend any more than forty today," I replied. I had no idea what there was to see, or how far away it was or how much was normal to pay for a taxi. I had six hours before I had to be back in port.

"Yes, yes, ok, come," he said.

The man's name was Madee. His English was workable but not brilliant, so after I asked him about himself and his family we soon settled into silence.

We drove down a long dual carriageway flanked by vendors selling statues, trinkets and more statues. Motorbikes weaved their way in between cars that drifted aimlessly across the lanes without a care in the world. The din of horns and the drone of small scooters blended into a constant hum of noise. Occasionally a field of water and mangroves would flash past, to be replaced again by statue vendors and intricately carved walls shielding small temples behind.

At one point we drove past ten statue shops, one after the other, selling exactly the same statues. It wasn't the last time I would see this phenomenon in Asia and I couldn't understand how it works. Someone must have walked down the street, past nine statue shops and thought, 'you know what this place needs? Statues.' How do all these shops stay in business? How often do people even buy statues?

We eventually reached a large temple. Madee parked the van and left me to have a look inside.

The noise of traffic disappeared as soon as I walked in. Straight ahead of me was a large, triangular shrine carved with snarling dragonheads and figures of human bodies with monkey heads, all set amongst intricate stonework. A path lead through the wall on my right and into another courtyard.

I wandered in and found a green fountain pond ringed by a mossy stone fence. A large stone in the centre of the pond was carved in the shape of a turtle. It had a tiny shrine resting on its shell, capped with a small thatch roof and overhung by branches from surrounding trees. The only sound was the gentle trickle of water spouting from the surface of the fountain.

Up until that point, I hadn't really grasped the idea that I'd left Australia. So far all I'd seen was ocean. But now I was here, suddenly standing in a temple in Bali. I looked around, listening to the sound of distant horns and breathing the hot, humid air.

Over the next two hours Madee took me to some shops (he'd obviously made a deal with the owners), but eventually I had enough of being ferried around so we headed back along the dual carriageway towards Benoa. Rain began to bucket down from above, flooding the road and sending motorcyclists scooting for cover. We pressed on through the heavy traffic, windscreen wipers hurrying back and forth. Then the rain stopped, almost as suddenly as it began and the sun emerged again when we pulled into the port.

"Ok, I said 50 dollars, but here you have given me 40,"

said Made.

"That's because I said 40." I replied.

"No, yes, but we agreed 50."

"Well, I have forty, like I said. All yours." I let myself out of the van.

The throng of drivers pressed in again.

"Yes, hello, where are you going?"

"I'm going for a walk." I pressed through and the moths flocked.

"To where? There is nowhere here. Where are you going?"

"Just for a walk."

I still had three hours to pass, so I broke out of the crowd, crossed a main road and headed down a side street flanked by ramshackle stores selling boat supplies and clothing. Men nodded, others waved a friendly hello. Tiny shacks sold food, breaking the smell of the dirty harbour beyond.

The road led to a dock. I stopped to admire the old, ramshackle wooden fishing boats. They were each twenty or so metres long with high painted prows that sloped back towards a small cabin. The colours were brilliant. Some were painted in bright blue, others in red, all crowded together. Some decks were filled with sleeping figures under makeshift canopies.

A teenage boy emerged from behind the cabin of a boat trapped deep in the milieu. Below my feet, brown water and floating garbage sloshed lazily against the coloured hulls.

"Is this your boat?" I asked.

He nodded, then turned and said something in Indonesian to someone out of my sight. He looked back at me and watched. Other boys started emerging from the back of the boat.

"What are your names?" I asked, carrying my voice

across the deck of a boat that floated between us. The first boy turned and yelled something again towards the cabin, then turned to face me. He pointed at the deck beneath his feet.

"Can I come?"

"Yes, yes," he said. More boys were filtering onto the deck to see what was going on. I clambered onto the boat between us and walked over the crumbling deck to where the two boats were bumping gently together. A group of seven boys were waiting for me, all teenagers, smiling and talking between themselves.

"You can speak English," I said to the boy. He had a pudgy look, narrow eyes set deep into his face and dark curly hair. He smiled and nodded.

"A little, yes."

"My name is Ewen." I pointed to myself. "What is your name?"

"John," he said and looked at his friends for support. They grinned at him.

"How do I ask in Indonesian?"

He said a flurry of words that I mimicked but can no longer remember. One by one the boys introduced themselves. I struggled to remember names so I took out my notebook and they all crowded closer. When I pronounced each name they would laugh, correct me then wrote their name in neat block letters. Taufik, Syahrul, Rama, Ares, Didi, Mail and John.

"Is John really your name?" I asked with a grin.

"Yes, yes," he replied. "John Andamany, my full name." The others grinned some more, staring at me.

Taufik, a lean boy with a big grin, took out his phone. "Photo?"

We all gathered around and grinned at the camera, then they slapped me on the back and offered to show me their cabin.

We walked past an engine room full of steaming pipes to a room at the back of the boat, no more than four square metres. A large shelf split the space in two. Laundry fluttered on the small deck behind us and a fuzzy TV played in the corner.

The boys ushered me in. I sat down and asked them questions, translated by John. They were waiting in port for three months while their engine was being repaired.

"Three months! What do you do while you wait?"

John shrugged.

"Listen to music," he said. He looked at his friends. They laughed again.

"Do you know bagpipes?" I looked around. They grinned at me. I mimicked a piper and the shape of the bagpipes with a hand. "Bagpipes?"

I took out my phone and played a song taken from one of my grandfather's old CDs, cupping my hand to amplify the sound. The wail only just rose above the noise of the working harbour.

The boys laughed. "Scottish music," John grinned. I nodded and chuckled. A splash sounded outside as someone threw a rope into the still water.

I spent a while there, swapping songs and asking more questions about their life. They were bass fishers and lived out at sea, casting nets all day. Someone's father, I wasn't sure whose, owned the boat. Every so often they would come back to Bali for repairs. None of the boys went to school.

Aware of overstaying my welcome, I stood to go. Although for a moment I was tempted to ditch the cruise and ask if they knew a way of getting to Malaysia, in the end I climbed ashore.

I walked towards what looked like a shop to find something to eat. A plump and friendly-looking woman came from the back and grinned when she saw me.

"Hello!" she said. "Where are you from?"

"Australia," I replied. "But I'm here on a cruise."

She laughed. "A cruise! But you are not old. Why are you on a cruise?"

I chuckled and explained my story.

"All the way to Switzerland?" she gasped. "Come, come, do you want to sit down?" We moved to the back of her shack. A low plastic table sat on a concrete floor underneath a bamboo roof, lit by white light from a single naked bulb. Pots lined the thin walls. A thin, mangy cat weaved between my legs when I sat down.

"This store, it is called a warung here. It's like a small store. So! Can you speak Indonesian?" the woman asked.

"No, none at all," I confessed. "Namasaya Ewen."

"Ah! You can speak a little! My name is Ni Madee. It is a common name here. Men are called Madee and women Ni Madee."

"Ni Madee," I repeated.

"And you are Eh-wen?" she asked, leaning forward slightly.

"Yoo-wen," I responded. "It looks like Eh-wen but you say it like yoo-wen."

"Ah! Yoo-wen!" She laughed and clapped again. "Would you like some lunch, Yoo-wen?"

Ni bustled off to the kitchen and came back shortly afterwards with a packet of folded paper and three tiny chicken drumsticks in sauce.

"It is spicy maybe for you, but you can try, it is not spicy for me but the West they do not like spice!"

I spoke with Ni for a long while, about my brothers, her children, my plans and she taught me more Indonesian. The cat wandered underneath the table while we spoke and settled to sleep near my feet.

—

The ship left Bali amid passing squalls of rain. I stood on deck watching the distant grey smears next to a young guy with a well-groomed beard. He turned towards me.

"How's it going?" he asked. "Did you have a good day in Bali?"

"Definitely," I replied. "Saw some temples and met a few locals. It was nice. Did you?"

"Yeah. Mostly went shopping with my dad. I've been to Bali before."

"Ah, cool. It's my first time here. Interesting place."

He paused for a second. "So I need to ask. Why are you here?"

"On this cruise?" I laughed. "Seems odd, doesn't it. I'm travelling to Asia, but I'm not allowed to fly. This was the only way to leave Australia without a plane."

"Without flying? Why? That's so expensive."

I shrugged. "It adds a challenge."

"You know you could fly to Singapore for like three hundred dollars?"

"Yeah, I definitely thought about it. But I'd regret it. How come you're here?"

A gust of warm air rushed past. "My dad wanted to go on a cruise and my mum hates boats," he said. "I got a free ticket."

"How are you finding it?"

He looked around quickly.

"Old," he said. "Very, very old. You?"

"The same. I'm Ewen and it's a relief to meet you."

He laughed and shook my hand. "Herarn. It's a relief to

meet you too!"

We spoke a while longer. Herarn was 27, from Perth. He had a major exam coming up and was using the cruise as an opportunity to study. It was more than a relief to meet him. I'd been looking at two weeks of almost total silence.

That evening I met Herarn at the dining room and was able to move my seat to his table, where I met the people with whom I'd be eating for the next nine days; Frank and Valda, who were retired, Francesco and Maria, a middle-aged Italian-Australian couple and Cary and Tracey, two salt-of-the-earth types. I didn't know it at the time, but our little group was to become tight-knit over the rest of the cruise.

The ship passed through the Lombok Strait overnight and sailed north towards Malaysia. The horizon was now an indistinct grey smudge circling the ship, the sea a dull and restless mirror of the overcast sky.

In the afternoon, while I was sitting in a chair reading my book, a man stopped next to me.

"Not studying, are you?" he asked loudly. I looked up. He was middle aged with close-shaven hair and painfully white teeth.

"No, no," I said. "I'm on holiday!"

"Good man. What brings you on the cruise anyway?"

"I'm on a trip," I replied. "But I'm not allowing myself to fly. Turns out this is the only way to leave Australia without an airplane."

He whistled softly. "Bit lonely though?"

"Yup."

"John." He stuck out a hand out. He was from Perth and travelling with his wife. We chatted for a time, mostly small talk that I can't remember, before he left me to read.

—

Morning light found us in Kelang, Malaysia. The cruise staff told us we were going to Kuala Lumpur, but it was an hour and half drive for $65. Port Kelang offered nothing of interest other than a shopping mall, although I did spend a good few hours watching the working port from the back of the ship. It was absolutely enormous, a huge canal long enough to fit multiple container ships lengthwise. Gigantic magnets lifted shipping containers from trucks then stacked them on the waiting vessels like the world's largest game of Lego. I hoped to see one drop and smash. None did.

The next port of call was the historic city of Georgetown in northern Malaysia. It seemed promising. I rose early and set off wandering the streets.

The ship had docked conveniently close to one of the main sights, a low-walled old stone fort called Fort Cornwallis. From there it didn't take me long to hit the old quarter – a maze of narrow alleys flanked by crumbling walls, tiled roofs and colourful wooden shutters. The streets were thronged with dreadlocked backpackers and mums in broad straw hats. Birds watched me cautiously from the melee of overhead power lines. Stray cats moved silently past the myriad potted palms arrayed outside the row houses, their skin sliding over protruding bones. The blanket of humidity amplified the occasional sickly-sweet smell of stagnant gutters.

I impulsively walked through a decorated gateway between two houses and came into a small courtyard. A Chinese-style temple sat at the other end. Intricately carved wooden columns supported its curved tile roofs. I was alone.

I scanned the courtyard, glanced behind me and then moved cautiously past the solid wooden doors into the temple. I wasn't sure if I was allowed to enter. Red drapes and lanterns hung from the rafters. The murky interior was lit only by candles, although a little bit of sunlight reflected from the courtyard through the narrow entranceway. There was a strong smell of incense.

I moved further in, checking left and right for anyone that might charge me an entrance fee, but nobody was there. A small gold statue sat watching me amongst smoking incense and gilded carvings. To the left a single pair of sandals sat at the foot of a wooden staircase. I took my shoes off and padded silently up the stairs. A monk reverently attended to the candles smoking softly around another gold figurine, so I waited on the terrace. The monk then violently hacked up some phlegm and shuffled into a side room.

A sign in English caught my eye. I was standing in the old home of the Kien Teik Tong, a secret mafia-type society that once controlled the surrounding neighbourhoods. A bricked-up passageway was evident on a nearby wall, which according to the sign led to the back of the shops on the street outside.

I stepped back onto the street and dodged a few mopeds to reach the Khoo Khangsi temple nearby. This was exactly like the one I'd just visited, except bigger and full of white people. I joined them (being white myself) and we all stared reverently at the intricate artwork. Large wet patches were visible on everyone's backs.

I made my way back to the cruise ship, waddling slowly to stop my sweaty skin from chafing. I had a long, cold shower, then lay on my bed mindlessly as BBC World gave me minute-by-minute updates on the weather in South America.

—

I woke up to a panoramic view of small islands dotted around the entrance to a tranquil bay, fenced by sheer mountainsides carpeted in jungle. Little fishing boats putted around and left trails of whitewash across the calm water. A small, rusted tanker was anchored a few hundred metres from the cruise ship. We'd docked at the island of Langkawi, near the border with Thailand.

Buses and a herd of taxi drivers milled around on the dock, evidently waiting to whisk us around the island. I thought of Madee and instead decided let my feet take me wherever they wanted.

I soon found there isn't much to Langkawi if you choose to see it on foot. I walked through a bustling little town filled with cashed-up tourists and duty-free shopping malls, then down a highway running alongside dry roadside fields. Oxen grazed on tufts of long grass. After a time, I turned off the road and walked past lots of holiday homes for rent, small resorts and over small dry canals filled with local fishing boats.

Sometime in the early afternoon I came to a beach. Jet-skis thumped across the water between jungled islands and tourists lounged in deck chairs nearby soaking up the hot tropical sun. I had stumbled into a resort.

I glanced around and made eye contact with a staff member, but he assumed I was just another guest and returned to reading his book. I decided to make the most of this discovery.

I found the pool, which was an enormous expanse of clear blue water shaded by canopies with attached jacuzzis and a waterfall. The cool water was a relief from the oppressing heat. I thought I caught a few sideways glances, but nobody bothered me. I was just another pale white guy enjoying his Malaysian holiday. Plus, I thought to myself, how would anybody find me out? "Excuse me, you there. You look a little too poor to be swimming here. What is your room number?"

The only issue was that all the other guests had resort-issued blue and white striped beach towels and I did not. I swam for a while longer, unwilling to leave the cool, shaded water, but soon I had to move on. This is when my lack of towel would identify me as a fraud. There was only one option. I got out of the pool and grabbed my bag, then in full view of the guests and staff members, walked out of the front of the resort shirtless and dripping wet.

That evening, back on the ship, Herarn and I were up on the deck at an outdoor party. I saw John and his wife and pointed them out to Herarn.

"Ever spoken to that guy?" I asked. "He's come up to me a few times."

"That's the guy that's been hitting on me!" Herarn exclaimed.

"What? The bald dude with his wife?"

"Yeah! I went to the LGBT meet-up and he was there and wanted my number. I'd seen him with his wife though so played it off, but it's been awkward ever since. I reckon he thinks we're a couple."

I looked at John, who had spotted us. He was giving Herarn and I a sullen look.

"You're kidding," I said. "He's married!"

"Apparently," Herarn replied, "but he won't leave me alone!"

Our final port of call was Phuket, Thailand, where we docked at a port with views similar to Langkawi. I had no map, so I wandered out of the port and turned left in the hope I'd come across somewhere noteworthy.

After a kilometre of walking along a jungle road I found a hotel, where an Australian guy told me that the city was ten kilometres in the other direction. I walked back out onto the road, disappointed, but then saw a place offering mopeds for $12 a day. Bargain. I signed some forms and set off towards Phuket City, excited by my newfound freedom.

Soon the traffic thickened and I found myself in a terrifying swirl of weaving mopeds, honking cars and cluttered signs. I followed the road into what seemed to be Phuket, parked the moped and thankfully discovered that I was right next to the old town.

Phuket, much like Georgetown, is an old colonial city with colourful row houses, archways and the occasional Chinese temple. I walked for some time down one coloured row and up another. Each row-house had a different colour – bright yellow, then sky blue, then red.

After admiring these I stopped for a cheap coffee to plan my next move. The Internet told me that Phuket is famous for an enormous Buddha statue on top of a hill. Intrigued, I walked back to my scooter and buzzed off.

I was adjusting to the rhythm of the road but it still took a lot of concentration to navigate the swirl of vehicles, so I was relieved to find that the Big Buddha was fairly well signposted. I turned off the main road and powered up a steep hill. Suddenly there were lots of white people in tuk-tuks. This was a clear indicator that I was going the right way.

The road climbed higher through a series of switchbacks. Not far up the hill I passed one stall offering elephant rides through the jungle. A baby elephant stood alone by the roadside, ignored by the handlers who were attending to some adult elephants nearby. I parked the moped and walked over for a closer look.

The baby elephant saw me as I approached and turned in my direction. It was only as tall as my waist and was covered in a thin layer of long orange hair, almost like an orang-utan. It became excited when I moved closer and walked towards me to say hello with its mouth smiling open, but was instantly jerked backwards. There was a chain wrapped around one of its front legs, no more than two feet long, that kept it anchored to the concrete.

The elephant tried moving towards me again but as soon as it lifted its leg the chain clinked and tightened mercilessly. Thwarted, the elephant pulled at the chain and reached its trunk towards me. Just when I was about to touch, a handler came around the corner. The elephant turned towards him, probably hoping for food, but he walked past. I returned to the moped and left in a sullen mood.

The big Buddha was just up the road and was, as advertised, big. He sits with his legs crossed, overlooking Phuket with a sleepy expression and gleaming white in the sun. Herds of sweaty tourists heaved themselves up the steps, past a number of construction workers still building the base of the Buddha. The figure itself was complete but its interior was a maze of concrete columns and dim construction lighting.

The views, however, were the real attraction. I could see Phuket lying under a dim smog, ringed by hills. To the south, the hills rolled away to a distant, hazy ocean, with islands lying offshore like enormous ships waiting at anchor.

Suddenly I realised I had no idea what the weather was doing in South America. I hurried back to the Sun Princess to find out. There were thunderstorms in Brazil.

We had one more day at sea. The ship slid slowly through the Straits of Malacca, the narrow waterway separating the Malay Peninsula from the Indonesian island of Sumatra. Land was visible on the horizon. Jellyfish bobbed in the ship's wake, drifting brainlessly by as behemoth ships ploughed their way in the opposite direction.

That night was my last dinner with Herarn and our tablemates. I had grown used to their company. It was, in a sense, a sort of home. A band struck up. I sang along.

3
THE ISLANDS

We disembarked in Singapore the next morning. I hoisted my pack and walked for the first time in almost two weeks. It was a Sunday morning, the streets were almost deserted, all my belongings were on my back and all of Asia lay at my feet.

In Singapore I met an old family friend named Kim, who lived in the apartment above ours when I was a toddler. We met near the Marina Bay Sands hotel, a gleaming trio of skyscrapers with what can only be described as an enormous ship curving across the top of all three, and after an excited hello we walked towards the new Gardens by the Bay.

The gardens are a lush jungle of rise enormous man-made 'trees', intricate lattices of steel, several stories high and covered in moss, ferns and ivy, that taper inwards before fanning out like a big leafy umbrella far above the tree tops. A swinging bridge curved between a few of them, high above the jungle canopy. It looked like the set to a Star Wars movie. Singapore never ceases to amaze me. It's a place where they just seem to get shit done.

Later that night we met Kim's husband Geoffrey for dinner. I grinned when I saw Geoff's long limbs striding their way towards our table.

"Geoff! Great to see you again," I said.

"What is on your face?" he replied incredulously, shaking my hand.

I laughed and stroked my beard. "I'm a backpacker now. Just want to look the part." He shook his head in disgust and chuckled.

I spent three days there catching up with Kim and Geoffrey. We went to the zoo, to a few more of Singapore's enormous shopping malls and to many restaurants to chat and catch up.

Over dinner one evening, Kim pulled found an old photo of my family that she'd kept. My brothers all looked cute, but I didn't. See, when I was small I had an extremely large skull. It was truly huge. My face was normally proportioned, but my hair just rose upwards from my forehead like a bearskin hat on a Buckingham Palace guard. The midwife must have pulled me out with an industrial-strength vacuum cleaner. To top this off, I was also afflicted by this weird thin-lipped smile. In every photo of me between the ages of four and eight I look like some kind of paedophilic alien. You know when new parents show off their child and you have to say 'oh wow, so cute!' even if it looks like something that's just crawled out of a swamp? I was one of those.

—

I eventually left Singapore on early morning bus across towards Malacca, an old trading town a few hours away. The first stop was the Malaysian border. After passing through customs, I walked back out to the car park and couldn't find the bus. It had completely disappeared. I stood there looking stupid until someone ran and led me gently back to where I was supposed to be. The driver then sat me in the front seat and forbade me from opening the curtains, so southern Malaysia just looked like linen.

Once we arrived in Malacca I caught a public bus into town and started looking for the place I'd booked. After wandering through the sticky heat for half an hour I eventually spotted the sign I was looking for on a long building covered in ads for face whitening cream. Two boys were grilling chicken kebabs on the street outside under a haze of blue smoke and circling insects. There was a narrow staircase just behind them. I plodded up.

I was greeted at the top by a small, bustling lady who introduced herself hurriedly as Linda. She ushered me into the kitchen. A grizzled old man sat there. He had no visible teeth and strips of colourful Band-Aids covering the left lens of his glasses. He grinned his gums at me, then groaned and gestured with his hands. Bugs flitted around a naked bulb above his head.

I glanced at Linda, who bustled me to my room - nothing more than a sunken mattress and weak wall fan. She then showed me the electric shower adjoining the kitchen. There was a clove of garlic next to the soap. An ant scurried along the floor.

I thanked Linda and decided to leave immediately to find dinner, settling for a street-side place just down the road. While I was eating the owner came to my table and said something incomprehensible. He pointed to my right, so I turned my head and saw another guy getting in a car. He grinned at me and waved.

I looked back at the owner. He smiled and walked back to his wok.

I eventually got up to pay.

"No, no, already pay," said the waiter. His black moustache wiggled enthusiastically.

"I haven't paid," I said, offering him the cash. Smoke drifted in from the grill outside.

"No, the man, he pay, the man he pay food," the waiter replied, gesturing to where the car had been parked. Suddenly it clicked.

"Ah! Right. Thanks. Well, tell him thanks. If he comes back. Thanks!"

I rose early the following morning and set off to wander around Malacca. It was once a big port town, but the river silted up and it's now a UNESCO World Heritage site. The centre of town has a number of old red Dutch-style buildings clustered next to the languid brown river that splits the town in two. A small, tacky windmill had been built nearby, to the never-ending joy of the busloads of Chinese tourists being dropped off next door. A gleaming new Hard Rock café sat across the river.

I set off for a walk down Jonker Street, Malacca's lantern-hung main strip, before splitting off to wander down side roads and alleyways. It was quiet. Deep gutters ran next to footpaths that weaved their way through small arches underneath the overhangs of houses, the long rows broken occasionally by small Chinese temples. The sun struck the tiled rooftops but the light had yet to reach the street, so it was still cool in the shade. Cats with bent tails slid between car tires and small birds flitted amongst the ever-present tangle of overhead power lines.

On that note, Malaysia just couldn't seem to do powerlines. This, I later discovered, was true of all of Southeast Asia. There was always an absolute clusterfuck of cables overhead, hundreds of wires running every which way off every pole like Silly String. It seemed like every individual appliance in each apartment had its own cable out to the street. I'm surprised the poles actually stood upright under the weight.

When the heat of the day had really set in, I stopped to sit on a bench to have a drink. A girl with dark hair stopped and wiped her forehead.

"Hot, isn't it?" she said.

"So hot," I replied. "I can only walk for about twenty minutes before I need to sit down." I gestured at the bench I was on.

She laughed and rubbed her eyes. "Same here."

"Want to sit?"

"Sure." She pulled a drink bottle out of her backpack and raised the bottle high. "I'm Kristina," she said.

"Ewen," I replied. "Nice to meet you. How long have you been in Malacca?"

"Just today. I came here from Singapore last night. I'm staying at this place, it is cheap, but there is nobody there. I have the room all to myself." She spoke with a thick German accent.

"I came from Singapore as well." I told her about the place I was staying.

She chuckled. "And how did you book this place?"

"AirBnB. Last time I do that in Asia."

"Yes," she said, standing up. "Well in my room I have two mosquitoes. I killed one last night but the other won't stop bothering me."

"Sounds like a strained relationship. Have you given it a name?"

"No," she laughed. "But maybe I call him Paul. I know an annoying guy called Paul. He is like this mosquito. Want to walk further?"

We talked while we wandered. Kristina was also travelling on her own after her boyfriend had to fly home to work and she had plenty of advice about travelling Asia.

We passed through twisting alleyways, past photorealistic street art and slinking cats, then down to the riverbank. Scores of dead fish floated in the flotsam. A large lizard slipped into the fetid water on the far side. Sickly sweet smells wafted in the air. The temperature was forty degrees in the shade and the humidity was almost 100%.

There were certainly nice parts of Malacca, but the heat and the sickly brown river made the place a fever. I was downing water and turning it straight into sweat. Kristina told me she was planning on heading to a place called Tanah Rata, in the Cameron Highlands, where she said the temperature didn't often rise above the low twenties. I agreed to go with her the next morning.

It was on my way to meet Kristina to catch the bus that I had my first encounter with an Asian toilet hose, also known as a 'poo gun'. It wasn't to be my last. I searched desperately, but the only bathroom I could find had squat toilets with leaky rubber tubes attached to taps on the wall. You get the drift. It was not pleasant.

—

Tanah Rata, as it turned out, was further north than Kuala Lumpur, meaning I'd later have to backtrack to see the city. I decided the cool weather was worth it and in any case, it was nice to let Kristina lead the way. She had been travelling in Asia for months and clearly knew what she was doing. It was all still new and a little scary for me.

She bought us two bus tickets and we were soon whisked away in an air-conditioned coach past the endless palm oil plantations that cover most of Malaysia. There were two other backpackers on the bus and we quickly struck up conversation.

"Cameron Highlands huh," the guy said. "Heard there's been some robberies up there."

"Robberies?" I asked.

"Yeah man. Like, dudes with machetes and shit. Stopping hikers in the hills and taking all their money, like, and shit."

We changed coaches late in the afternoon and settled in for a windy trip up into the mountains. The road snaked past sheer cliffs of rock with trees perched precariously above. Palls of smoke rose above the canopy where men were back-burning the jungle. One fire was right next to the road. The line of low flames flickered in the growing darkness. As the sun dropped, long thin clouds far above the tree-covered mountains glowed a vivid orange in mimicry of the fires below.

After a few wobbly hours we arrived in total darkness in Tanah Rata. I could see no signs indicating where we were but Kristina was convinced we'd arrived, so I followed her lead. We heaved our packs out of the belly of the bus and struck off down a side road in search of a hostel Kristina had researched beforehand.

Soon the buildings ran out, the din of mopeds and traffic dropped to nothing and the thick trees pressed in ominously on either side of the thin road. Mysterious sounds clicked and rustled in the darkness. A glow of flames stained the sky somewhere far off, but the only other light was from our phones. Every rustle in the bush became a machete-wielding bandit.

"I'm glad you're here," Kristina chuckled, but not without quick glances to either side. Her phone flashed in the darkness, revealing thick jungle that shrank in the light, before quickly growing back to size when she turned to face the road again.

"Well I'm glad you're here," I said. "We are going the right way, aren't we?"

She checked her phone. The light was glaring in the jungle.

"Yes, I think," she said quietly, glancing around again.

We pressed on and up a small hill where eventually an archway with the name 'De Native Hostel' emerged from the darkness. A narrow, rutted pathway led up a deep cleft flanked by steep sides of thick jungle. A silent crowd of trees watched our approach. A movement in my peripheral vision made my snap my head to the side, but the darkness went still again.

"It's like the start to a horror movie," Kristina whispered. A bead of sweat slid down my forehead and stung my eye.

The trees were silent.

As it turns out, all that suspense was for nothing. It was a real hostel, complete with a campfire and a herd of Germans. One main building was set in a clearing, flanked by four little bamboo huts in a row like a mother duck leading her ducklings. Dogs with thick bellies slept on the grass and a puppy whimpered in the dark.

We paid a shirtless, stoned French guy for our beds then settled in to meet the other backpackers around the campfire. Their names are gone now, but the conversation didn't die until far into the night.

—

The next day we agreed to go on a walk through some tea plantations with some others from the hostel. We stood by the side of the road flagging cars, hoping to get a lift to the start of the trail. Eventually a man in a pick-up pulled over and we got in the back and sped off.

He dropped us at the start of the trail in the next town over. We climbed steadily up a hill as a group, following the trail that weaved its way through the thick jungle undergrowth. The air was cool and gentle breezes swayed the top of the trees. A few birds sang here and there: some melodious, some harsh and cackling.

After two hours or so we made it to the summit. The view stretched far over steep, jungled hills to a hazy horizon, which we took a moment to enjoy before setting off in a long, straggled convoy down the paved road that led back towards town.

The road soon turned a bend and revealed the view we'd walked all this way for – the famous tea plantations. Everyone stopped in awe. We were standing at the top of a long valley that sloped down before rising again to a hill on the far side. A green carpet of tea plants arranged in neat rows, no more than knee height, blanketed the steep, humped mounds that rose and fell towards the distant hill.

It was like I'd walked into a Tetley's commercial. Birds flitted among the rows of tea plants and insects droned lazily in the gentle sunlight that dappled the green, rolling hillocks. Small streams gurgled next to the road before striking off along secret paths underneath the rows of tea. It was as if the landscape was sleeping and someone had thoughtfully draped a striped green blanket on top. We walked further, every turn of the road revealing distant hills blanketed in more tea and small streams of water.

Kristina left early the next morning for Penang with a few others, leaving me sitting alone at the hostel. The repeated goodbyes were already beginning to wear a little and I was only a few weeks in. Yet sitting around wasn't going to help my mood, so I bought a bus ticket to Kuala Lumpur and left that afternoon.

I spent the rest of the day doing some life administration, like washing clothes and replacing my recently deceased headphones, then wandered the city streets.

I liked Kuala Lumpur. If Singapore is a clean, ordered and sanitary vision of the future, then KL is the opposite: dirty, gritty, hectic, noisy, smoky and completely chaotic. Smoke wafted upwards from clamorous street stalls and bustling people towards monorail trains that slid along concrete tracks high above. Hawkers peddled all kinds of junk in their neon-lit shops and swarms of mopeds buzzed along the street and up the footpath underneath signs that littered the high buildings flanking the street like cliffs over a valley, advertising clubs, brothels, massages, doctors, hostels and skin whitening creams. Enormous TV screens lit up hazy intersections and loud music blared from dozens of different places. It was an assault of noise, light, smoke, people, traffic and the energy was infectious. I had the impression (and not for the first time on this trip) that I'd landed on another planet.

—

I intended to go to the Batu Caves, apparently a must-do in Kuala Lumpur, so the following morning I caught the monorail, marvelled some more at the city as I glided through, then got on a train out to the caves on the outskirts of the city.

The first thing I saw was an enormous cliff face rising from the trees near the station. I followed the crowd along its base and was soon greeting by a similarly enormous golden Buddha, standing upright with one hand raised as if he was peacefully directing traffic.

A long staircase led up a steep slope towards the cliff behind the Buddha. Tourists of varying levels of fitness plodded upwards. Some paused on the intermittent landings to gasp and wheeze. Small monkeys darted around our feet to grab discarded water bottles and scamper off.

At the top, the staircase flattened out and led into a huge cavern, well over twice the height of the tallest cathedrals. It dwarfed the tourists that gazed upwards around me. Gaudy neon lights decorated shrines around the cave floor and shrill Malaysian music blared from nearby speakers. Pigeons fluttered in the dark heights. At the top, small holes in the cavern's roof allowed shafts of light to pierce the darkness that clung resolutely to the base of big icicles of rock.

It was large, I'll give it that, but the blaring music and flashing neon had turned the place into a tacky attraction. It was a shame really, because it was truly enormous and might otherwise have left a lasting impression.

—

An urge to keep moving saw me on a train the next day to Butterworth, which is just across the water from Georgetown (where the cruise docked the week before). I was planning on catching a connection straight to Thailand but this plan was thwarted as soon as I got off the train. A backpacking couple were asking directions from a local and called me over.

"Hey," the guy said. "Do you know how to get to Georgetown?"

"I think there's a ferry," I replied. "But I'm not sure. Is there a ticket office around?"

"We think there's one over there," said the girl. "Maybe we should just check it out Max."

Max looked to where she was pointing as she turned back to me. The platform was now deserted.

"Sorry! Should've introduced myself first. I'm Maisie and this is Max." Maisie stuck out a hand.

"Ewen. And Max, was it?"

"Yeah, nice to meet you Ewen," Max said. "What are your plans?"

"Well, I was hoping to find a connection to Thailand, so I'll come to the ticket place with you."

"Sorted then!" Max said, hoisting his pack.

The ticket counter wasn't far away.

"Hi," I said. "Hat Yai? Thailand?"

The lady shook her head and pointed at the board. There was nothing running until tomorrow.

"You could come with us," Max suggested. "Get

something in Georgetown maybe."

"If you're alright with that?"

"Yeah! Of course, it'll be great to have you."

We caught the ferry over and arrived not far from where the Sun Princess had docked the week before. We then spent ages trying to hail a taxi. Taxis are one of those funny things that are everywhere when you don't need one and nowhere when you do. There always seemed to be flocks of seedy-looking men with small eyes and thin moustaches squawking 'taxi, taxi!' all over Malaysia, but as soon as we actually needed a lift they'd all flown back to their nests. What's with that?

We eventually found a hostel, dropped our stuff and set off exploring. We visited a few places I'd been before – the Khoo Khangsi temple and a few of Georgetown's famous street murals. The temperature was still over 40 degrees. We had to stop every ten minutes and just stare at the ground with fluid leaking from our faces.

Maisie suggested that we drop into a mosque to have a look and cool down. As we walked into the compound, a middle-aged man with a vivid orange neck beard approached and offered to give us a tour.

He instructed us to remove our shoes and gave Maisie a shawl, then led us into the mosque and began speaking about Islam. The air inside was less dense and the marble floor was cool under our bare feet.

The mosque itself was interesting, but I couldn't stop wondering how this guy dyed his facial hair. It was the colour of orange dishwashing liquid. He'd also shaved it into a strange shape. Picture two S-shaped lines of hair coming down from his ears and meeting in a goat-like orange tuft, almost like an orangutan clinging desperately to his chin.

He spoke at me suddenly. "Do you believe in Adam and Eve?"

I made eye contact. There was a long pause while I pictured him dunking his chin in a can of paint.

"Brother. Do you believe in Adam and Eve?"

I blinked. "What? Uh... yeah? I know the story?"

He made a manic grin and began listing other Muslim practices like fasting, prayer, abstinence during Ramadan and circumcision. He spoke for a particularly long time about this last topic.

"It is much cleaner, yes brothers?" He gave Max and I another grin, showing both rows of teeth. We looked at each other and quickly made for the exit.

"Come to Langkawi with us," Max said while we tucked into cold ice creams later that
day. "I don't know how long we'll be there, but you can get ferries on to Thailand."

"I'd love to, but..." I trailed off. Time flew far faster with Max and Maisie than it did when I was alone. "How much are the ferries?"

Max pulled out his phone to have a look. The ferries running at this time of year were expensive and infrequent. I'd already been to Langkawi and felt the pressure of time.

"I really would love to..."

"It's alright," Maisie interjected. "If you've gotta go, you've gotta go. Just do you, wherever you need to be."

"Yeah. I've just... got a lot further to go, you know, and I'm not sure how much time I'll need. I wish I could."

"So you'll head to Thailand?" Max asked. "Do you know where?"

"Not yet. I was thinking one of the islands but I'm not sure which."

"Well if you're after something quiet, we went to Ko Lanta. It's off the west coast. It was really cool, super chill. You'll like it."

"Oh right," I said. "Sounds like my kind of place. Hard to get to?"

"No, not at all. You can probably find a connection in Hat Yai."

There was a brief silence.

"Do you know when you'll be in Australia?" I asked.

"Not exactly," said Maisie. "But we'll let you know."

"Cool and let me know where! Maybe we can meet up again."

—

We said goodbye the next morning on the street outside the hostel. I hesitated after giving them both a hug, looking for more words to say. I struggled to find any and in the end said a quick goodbye and walked in the opposite direction, plunging back into the silence.

I crossed chaotic roads teeming with mopeds and walked over poorly kept flowerbeds towards the bus stop. I hurried into a nearby toilet, but once again, it was paperless. What a disappointment.

I found a minivan and settled into the mindless void of long distance trips as we drove towards the border, staring out the window without seeing anything much at all.

The van left Malaysia and entered Thailand without much trouble. Further along the same street, however, we were stopped at a military checkpoint. I decided to read about Thailand's southern provinces in my guidebook.

As it turned out, the region is home to a long running Muslim insurgency. Some 12,000 insurgents are fighting 150,000 Thai soldiers in a conflict that has killed thousands of people since 2004. Let me give you some choice quotes: "Mobile phone signals are jammed to prevent the insurgents using them to set off bombs"; "Barely a day goes by without a member of the Thai security forces being killed or wounded"; "An Australian study found that 5% of global terror attacks between 2002 and 2009 occurred in Thailand's Deep South."

I swallowed nervously and looked out the window. All I could see was a convenience store and a lot of people eating nuggets in a KFC.

After a two-hour layover in Hat Yai, the region's main town, I was whisked away in another minivan, then randomly changed vans once again on a busy highway before continuing on.

Late that night I arrived in Ko Lanta. I'd booked a hostel built on stilts over the water for three nights. It was run by a young guy that spent most of his days watching martial arts on a crackling TV. The place was made entirely of wooden planks, heavy tree trunks and a lot of rope. Out the back he'd suspended nets over the water, where I spent hours lying and watching fisherman on small skiffs putter out of their moorings in some hidden jungle creek towards the hazy sea.

Ko Lanta is a quiet place, exactly like Max and Maisie had promised, that is far removed from the full moon parties Thai islands are famous for. I spent most of my time there around the hostel, small-talking with other guests and reading my book, or motoring around the island and turning my unprotected arms deep shades of red.

—

One day I decided to go on a tour to some nearby islands. I joined twenty other tourists in the morning and we were squashed on to a small boat with an engine that sounded like a flabby fart, which took us out from Ko Lanta and motored steadily towards some distant specks of green.

The specks grew slowly from small lumps near the horizon to green thumbs in the middle distance, before finally revealing themselves to be islands of enormous cliffs jutting straight out of the sea, hundreds of metres into the air, like great ancient spearheads dropped from the clouds. Birds circled around the trees crowning the heights. It was a scene straight out of a postcard.

We snorkelled around a bit in the morning, saw some coral and some colourful fish and had lunch on a beach packed with other tour groups. The boat farted off again after lunch, taking us past islands with huts on stilts nestled against the sheer rock. I could just make out the inhabitants staring at our small wooden boat. They were sea gypsies, the guide said, who hardly ever set foot on land.

The boat stopped next to another island that looked much the same as the ones we'd visited that morning. It resembled a huge ship adrift that was being slowly reclaimed by trees and tangled jungle. On the guide's instructions we donned lifejackets and jumped overboard.

The guide swam ahead and led us under an overhang on the cliff face. A tunnel curved off to the right. We followed the guide further into the tunnel and soon it was totally dark save for the light from his torch. A string of women in burkinis passed the other way, lit intermittently by flickering torchlight, all clutching on to each other in a row like a floating Islamic caterpillar. Their chattering voices echoed loudly off the closing walls.

A light at the far end illuminated a wall of rock where the tunnel curved to the right again. We swam around and out into a small lagoon and beach set at the bottom of a deep circular well in the ground. It was no more than 30 metres in diameter and surrounded entirely by enormous cliffs.

We milled about, staring up at the jungle peeking curiously over the rim of cliffs high above. It was a perfect pirate's cove - which as it turns out, is exactly what it was once used for. It's called the Marakot Cave. Nobody had been able to take cameras through the tunnel, so we milled around uncertainly for a while before swimming back into the darkness.

From Ko Lanta I caught a ferry back to the mainland, another couple of vans and an overnight train to Bangkok. I rode in poverty class - crowded wooden benches, open windows and a lot of click clacking noise. Palm trees and smallholdings flashed past as the sun dropped in the distance. A woman intermittently walked up and down the aisle yelling incoherently and carrying a plate of what looked like dried foreskins. I passed a few fun hours showing a small girl how to throw paper airplanes, then closed my eyes and attempted to sleep.

I had begun to draw up a rough plan in my head for the next few weeks. I had a lot of interest in going to Myanmar on the advice of a friend who had been a few years before. There was a border crossing close to Bangkok that would take me to Myanmar's south coast, a region that had only recently opened to foreigners. From there I would head north to the famous plains of Bagan, an ancient city of temples sprawled along the banks of the Irrawaddy.

I arrived in Bangkok on the morning of my birthday and found that the Burmese embassy was closed. There was a hostel just up the road from the embassy. I was quickly welcomed in by the owner, who introduced himself as Angkrit, and a few regulars who had clearly been there a long time. We got on well and they were kind enough to organise a group to go out for dinner that evening for my birthday. And so, within hours of arriving in Bangkok I found myself being sung to by people

I'd never met.

I dropped my passport and application off at the embassy the next morning and discovered I wouldn't be able to get it back until the following Monday. This left me with six unplanned days in Bangkok.

I took in the sights slowly - the temple complex of Wat Pho one day, Chinatown the next, wandering aimlessly through aromatic covered markets another. During one of these walks an old Thai guy with a wide smile stopped me on the street, just outside the walls surrounding a gleaming marble temple.

"Hello! Hello! Big beard! Nice beard!" He hurried over.

"Thanks! I grew it myself."

"Very good, very good, very red. Where you from?"

"Australia," I said.

"Australia, very nice, my name Tom." He stuck out his hand.

"Ewen," I said, shaking it.

"Ewen, do you know this temple? Very famous. I show you temple. I teach you about Buddhism."

He went on to assure me that he didn't want money - he was retired and simply wanted something to do with his time. I agreed. We walked in and he brought me over to a large gong and handed me a mallet.

"Now you must tell Buddha you are here. Knock on his door!"

I gave the gong a good whack and shattered the silence inside the temple. Tom then beckoned me towards a large drum, which I dutifully gave another whack. He then asked me to ring a shrill bell.

Tom then took me up to the main prayer hall, where

several locals were engaged in serious and silent prayer in front a large golden statue of Buddha. He walked me over to a stone bowl next to the statue.

"Come here, come here," he said, flicking water at my face. "Holy water. Now Buddha keeps you safe on the road."

Once I'd had a good look around, Tom invited me to follow him to see another sight down the road. I was enjoying his company and saw no reason to say no. Unfortunately the sight turned out to be a suit shop. This was a disappointing outcome. I was forced to spend the next fifteen minutes explaining to the shopkeeper why I didn't want to buy a suit.

"Excuse me, but I noticed that you're not buying that suit. Why is that?"

"Well I don't want a suit."

"Yes, but maybe you'll need a suit next week."

"Then I'll buy a suit next week."

"But what if your brother wants a suit?"

"My brother lives on the other side of the world."

"Yes, but what if he wants a suit? This suit is really very good. You should really buy this suit."

"He doesn't want me to mail him a suit."

"But look at this list of other people who have bought suits."

"I don't care. I said I don't want a suit."

"But what about this other suit?"

Eventually he got the message and let me be. I parted ways with Tom.

Soon my passport was ready, leaving me with one more night. Angkrit organised another dinner out, a Vietnamese pot-luck, and so my time in Bangkok came to an end exactly as it started – a street-side dinner with a group of people who had only just met, chatting like we'd known each other for years and likely to never get together again. And, for the first time, I found myself content with that. Time was passing too fast to allow upcoming goodbyes to throw long shadows.

4
The Lake

I left Bangkok on an early morning train towards Kanchanaburi, home of the famous Bridge on the River Kwai. The train passed through a shantytown built perilously close to the tracks, the closest rooftops only a foot or two from the train, then out into countryside. Lots of dust blew in through the windows and stung my eyes. I was pleased to discover that my beard was now long enough to wave slightly in the wind when I stuck my face out the window.

The train took three hours to get to Kanchanaburi. I put my pack on and went to get off, but a crowd of small, middle-aged Chinese ladies decided they wanted to board as soon as possible.

I tried to push forward but they surged on relentlessly in a tidal wave of self-importance. We became trapped in the narrow corridor between carriages, pressed together like battery hens and none of them were moving. One stood and grinned at me, resolutely blocking the open space in the next carriage. I gestured at her to move backwards but she was clearly happy to just wedge us all in.

We all stood there for about a minute, motionless and silent as they refused to concede an inch to let me off the train. One woman had jammed herself so solidly between my pack and the wall that her face resembled a soggy hot dog. I looked at them, they looked at me and I gestured again for them to make room but they didn't.

I bent my knees, leaned forward and pushed, sending every reserve of strength into my thighs. Soggy Hot Dog was dragged unceremoniously along the wall and the woman blocking the neighbouring carriage was shoved backwards when one of her friends fell into her. I paused to recover while the chattering grew louder and then steadied myself for a second effort.

Their voices rose in a unified panic when I heaved forward again. The energy built as I strained and after a brief but tense, quivering pause, I finally exploded out of the train and the small Chinese ladies cartwheeled helplessly through the air.

On a more sombre note, the train I took to Kanchanaburi runs along tracks known as the Death Railway. It was built during World War 2 by Allied prisoners – mostly British, Australian and Dutch - as well as 180,000 enslaved Asian workers. Over 100,000 people died building the railway.

I stood on the Bridge, which was now covered in other tourists and small groups of monks crossing the river. Each of the iron spikes holding the rails down on the wooden sleepers had a unique shape, warped by the hammer blows that sunk it into the wood. Some weren't hammered in properly and jutted resolutely out above the others.

The Bridge over the River Kwai is not a tall bridge, or a long one. In fact, it looks like most railway bridges the world over. But I thought I could see bloodstains on the iron.

I returned to the station to continue towards the Burmese border. I was ushered onto a van that took a winding route through increasingly remote villages, climbing steadily higher into the mountains. The jungle up here was entirely burnt away, making for an eerie post-apocalyptic landscape of black, shrivelled trunks and stained brown grass.

After two hours we came to a small gathering of low wooden houses that seemed to be the border.

I got out of the van and went through Thai customs without any problems. The only issue, however, was that the Thai and Burmese border posts were separated by seven kilometres of no man's land and the driver wasn't coming with us.

A man approached, who I recognised from the line at customs.

"Hallo, my name is Joel," he said, extending his hand.

"Ewen," I replied.

He looked around us. "Eet looks like ve have a petit problem! Maybe ve can get a leeft?"

We stood in the shade of an awning and after only a few unsuccessful attempts we were able to flag down a pick-up truck.

The road soon turned to dirt, shaking the frame of the pick-up and creating a cloud of dust that drifted lazily through the burnt jungle. Eventually we passed a small camouflaged wooden shack protected by a low wall of sandbags and arrived in a ramshackle village somewhere in the middle of the mountains.

One of the huts was an immigration post. Once we were processed, the next issue was to find a lift to the nearest town, a place called Dawei. Joel quickly found a guy who was willing to take us for a decent price. We got in his car alongside a young couple and their small baby and started bumping violently along more potholed dirt roads through endless kilometres of what must have once been lush jungle, but was now just a burnt-out black and brown memory. The driver kept a steady wail of Burmese pop music blaring through the car speakers.

Mid-afternoon we were forced to stop on the edge of a steep embankment that dropped to a swift-flowing river far below. A tree had fallen across the road. It was a huge thing and despite the efforts of around thirty men that had gathered there, it wouldn't budge at all. There was no way around it.

Joel and I settled in to wait and see what would happen.

Trucks packed with people clinging on the back pulled up behind our car and the crowd grew steadily over the next few hours.

As I was debating the relative merits of sleeping upright in the car or flat on the ground beside it, the woman sharing our 'leeft' strode towards me and thrust her baby into my arms. I was confused, to say the least, and the baby seemed just as confused as I was because he stared at me with huge eyes and an open mouth.

His mother then took out a phone and started taking pictures. I stood there holding the baby while he grabbed my beard with his tiny little hands. I tried to make some baby noises at him, but he just looked at me like I was a moron and continued searching for my chin.

Eventually a man showed up with a chainsaw and soon had the tree cut into moveable pieces. We bumped along for many long, juddering hours in the growing darkness until we eventually arrived in Dawei.

The city had no power. Joel and I wandered the black, empty streets searching for a hotel using the lights from our phones. We eventually found one and split a room for the night. I was planning on catching a train early the following morning - only ten hours away – so we had a quick dinner and went to bed.

—

I woke the receptionist at four to call a moped, which soon arrived to whisk me through a thin fog to a small, colonial building next to one platform. An old rusty train sat waiting on the tracks.

I was quickly ushered into a room and greeted by a man in tatty uniform sitting behind a wooden desk. Several other men sat on bags of grain stacked against the walls on either side and others came and stood at the open door that led onto the platform.

"Mawlamyine?" I ventured, glancing around at the silent group.

"Class?"

"Uh, cheap class. Second."

He looked up from the paper. "Not first? Ordinary class is..." He tapped the desk.

"Yes, no problem."

He laughed and said something to the others, prompting a chuckle around the room.

I boarded the train and made myself as comfortable as possible on one of the wooden benches in 'Ordinary Class', which was, as promised, extremely ordinary. The train whistled and set off in almost total darkness.

I had been warned that this train was slow, but I didn't realise how slow. It was actually so slow that it was possible to jump off for a wee then run and catch back up. The rails were almost completely covered by the encroaching jungle. The train pushed its way through, whipping branches at people's faces through the permanently open windows, and bounced and rocked violently while it chugged along the uneven rails. I could see the whole crowd of heads in my carriage rhythmically rise in unison, almost a foot in the air, then drop back down on the wooden benches with a spine-compressing thump.

The scenery was stunning. Temples poked shyly out of the morning mist, storks flapped upwards out of flooded rice paddies and behind it all the sun floated slowly upwards, a low ball of fire that occasionally slanted through a distant valley to light the mist a soft orange.

I was sharing a bench with a few children. The older

two were quiet but the youngest boy immediately focused all his attention on me. He was holding a bag of what looked like wedges of uranium and a bag of pink salt.

The boy turned to me and started yelling at me in Burmese, then thrust a wedge towards my mouth. It looked like a standard potato chip that you'd get with a burger, except extremely wrinkled and glowing a radioactive yellow.

I couldn't say no, not to this little fiend, so I took it warily and bit off a chunk. Funnily enough it actually tasted like a slice of nuclear waste – extremely sour yet also painfully spicy. I could feel my teeth melting.

The boy yelled at me again, grabbed my hand and thrust my uranium into the bag of crystallised thallium. He then pushed my hand back towards my mouth and gave me a look like he'd castrate me if I didn't eat it. I swallowed it quickly in case it burnt a hole straight through the bottom of my face. Satisfied with his work, the kid snatched my phone and started playing games while I checked to see if I'd grown a third nipple.

Over the course of the day the train wheezed to a wobbly stop in small villages of thatched bamboo huts built on stilts. Chickens pecked their way around small, fenced yards covered in brown fronds and men led herds of thin cows to pasture. People took the opportunity to load and offload supplies at each stop, so our carriage was soon piled high with boxes of vegetables and soft drinks. Uranium Boy left at one of these stops, leaving me with an English-speaking policeman named Jo-Jo and his elderly mother, who were both on their way to Mawlamyine.

Jo-Jo took great interest in my trip. As we spoke his mother grabbed some ingredients from a bag and quickly made me a pot of hot rice and mysterious chunks of bone. Jo-Jo kept me well provisioned and insisted on buying me bottled water and nuts at several stops. At one point an elderly man seated nearby tapped my shoulder and insisted I drink some sort of yellow alcohol, which looked like urine but thankfully tasted like pineapple.

I seated myself in the doorway and watched the sleepers flash past under my dangling feet while the sun started to drop over the far side of square paddies and wooden huts. The jungle rolled by, occasionally breaking to reveal sunken riverbeds and gurgling water, then closed again in a green curtain of tangled vines and leaves.

After a full twenty-four hours on the same train I finally arrived in Yangon. It was the early morning and I had a day to wander around the city. First, however, I needed to change and brush my teeth.

After a short walk I found a Shangri-La hotel. The doorman led me to the check-in desk.

The receptionist scanned me from head to toe. "Hello sir. Are you here to check in?" she said politely.

"I will in a moment. Could you just point me to the bathroom first?"

"Of course. Just around the corner, sir."

I walked in to the bathroom, dropped my pack on the marble floor and proceeded to wash my head, shampoo my beard, brush my teeth and change my clothes. I then hoisted my pack again and walked back into the lobby, past the receptionist and waved a cheery 'thanks!' on the way out.

I was intent on seeing the Schwedagon Pagoda, an enormous golden Buddhist shrine somewhere in Yangon. I didn't know where it was but I did have a local area map on my phone that could tell me where I was and what direction I was facing. All the place names were in local script, so I decided to aim for a large circular area at the junction of many roads on the basis that you can't make ten roads intersect around a great big circle and not put something interesting in the middle. My guess was correct and it wasn't long before I saw the top of the pagoda sticking upwards above the treeline.

A pagoda, or stupa, is essentially a huge spire made of gold that looks a bit like an upside-down ice cream cone. The Schwedagon Pagoda is the holiest Buddhist site in Myanmar and is the largest and most arresting pagoda out there. It's 100 metres tall, completely covered in gold, crowned with 5448 diamonds, 2317 rubies and a 76-carat diamond at the tip.

I arrived at the base of the pagoda and looked up, squinting at the glare reflecting off the gold surface. Other tourists padded around in bare feet, occasionally pausing to tilt their heads backward and try and see the immeasurable wealth high above. The only trouble, I thought, with crowning a 100-metre tall spire with thousands of precious gems is that they are too high to see.

I returned to the train station to catch the train to Bagan. Signs in the ticket area instructed locals to 'warmly welcome and take care of tourists'. One man seemed to have taken this message to heart because he asked to see my ticket then abruptly took my pack and strode off towards the train.

I scurried after him, insisting that I could take it, but he powered on and dropped it in my compartment. I thanked him profusely. He looked at me with a warm smile and stuck out his hand.

"Four thousand kyat," he said. Kyat is pronounced 'chat'.

"But I didn't ask you to take my bag," I said.

"Four thousand."

My frustration grew. "I'm not giving you any money! You can't just walk up to me, take my bag and then ask me for money afterwards. That doesn't make sense. I didn't need help, I didn't want help and so I'm not paying for help."

He didn't speak English. "2000 kyat."

I let out a breath of air. "No. I'm not giving you any money. Please leave."

He wiggled his hand. "2000 kyat."

I stuck five hundred in his hand. "I didn't agree to pay you before you picked up my bag, so this is all I'll give." I pointed at the door.

He rolled his eyes and left the train in a huff.

I'd booked a sleeper compartment, determined to get a flat bed and a half-decent sleep after the previous train. Two flat padded shelves sat above two sets of opposing chairs that flattened out into lower bunks. A small toilet was attached, which was really just a tiny cupboard with a hole in the floor.

I settled in and started reading my book. Others would soon join me. I imagined who they might be and for whatever reason pictured two or three American men with names like Kyle and Brad.

I was wrong. Two young women with Welsh accents entered the carriage.

"Hi! I'm Ewen," I said, perhaps too excitedly. I hadn't had a good conversation in fluent English since leaving Bangkok.

"Hi! I'm Sarah," one replied, sticking out her hand.

"And I'm Amy," said the other.

"How long have you been in Myanmar?" I asked.

"This is our first day actually," Sarah said. "We just flew in this morning from Bangkok. I've already been bitten by a dog." She showed me some green bruises on her upper arm.

"Ouch." I leaned over to have a closer look. "How did that happen?"

Amy groaned. "She likes dogs."

"I do like dogs," Sarah said. "I reached over to pat one and it jumped up and bit me."

"Have you got rabies?" I asked.

She laughed. "I think so. Every new feeling I have I'm convinced is a symptom."

We introduced ourselves while the train sat idling on the tracks. They were sisters and Amy was visiting Sarah, who worked in Bangkok. They'd decided to come to Myanmar for a week.

The sun treated us to a stunning display while we chatted. Streaks of purple, red and orange clouds stretched towards us from the horizon - a messy and dramatic finger painting of vivid colours over an ancient landscape. Dirt tracks, scored deep by the wheels of farmers' wagons, wound between dry fields on the way home to small villages of semi-collapsed thatched huts. It was the dry season and the land was dusty, but the fields were still bordered by green jungle. Every so often the train startled a stork into flight from a waterlogged paddy, until night fell and the view vanished.

—

I woke before the others and spent some time watching the sun climb over the other horizon. The train rocked from side to side on the warped rails. The sunrise was far softer than the sunset, a light hue of pink on the land's edge that blended into the dark blue above. The land had completely changed overnight. It was even drier, sandier and dustier. The tangled jungle was gone, replaced by strands of lone, thirsty trees on the edges of empty brown fields.

At noon, the train came to a wheezing stop at Bagan. We found a lift into town, checked into a hotel and promptly began exploring.

Bagan is split into two parts – the old town amongst the temples and a newer town a few kilometres away. We were staying in the new town, which lies on the bank of the mighty Irrawaddy River, although it was the dry season so the river was a lot less mighty than it would be in the monsoon.

We hired some electric scooters and followed the road leading towards the old town. After a time, a dirt track leading to a large brick temple opened on our right. We followed it to an empty, crumbling pagoda. We were hesitant, but there was no sign saying the pagoda was off-limits. We left our shoes on the steps at the entrance and walked in.

It took a moment for my eyes to adjust to the gloom. We'd walked into a small, dark room, occupied by a man sitting cross-legged against the wall. He was selling paintings arrayed on the floor. As the darkness receded I could just make out some faded murals on the walls, the images broken by exposed brick underneath as the temple slowly crumbled.

"Hello, where you from?" The man's voice abruptly brought life into the room.

"Australia," I replied.

"And Wales," said Sarah.

"Ah, UK people," the man said. "You like Bagan?"

"It's lovely," said Amy. "The temples are amazing!"

"Thank you. This here, very old temple. You can see here, there are old paintings, very old. Nobody fix them. This temple was left and is now becoming very old."

He stood up and moved to the wall, indicating the faint

lines with his hand. "They paint Buddha, paint the past. Good painters, you see here."

"They are."

"It is possible to go upstairs. But staircase is very steep, you must be careful." He pointed behind us at a narrow, dark doorway in the corner.

I ducked the low archway and climbed a steep flight of worn stone steps that opened out onto the roof and a low view over the plain. The bricks were warm beneath my bare feet. Dozens of shrines, twenty to thirty metres high, were scattered amongst the brown fields nearby. In the distance, an enormous dark monolith towered above the green treeline and dwarfed the spires around.

"What's it like?" Sarah called after me.

"Good!" I called back. "Come on up!"

The bricks of the pagoda were slowly separating, worn away by rain, giving me the impression that the place could topple at any moment like a huge Jenga stack. I walked around the spire through narrow archways and sideways through skinny, dark corridors. It was an ancient place, like an old man exhausted by the effort of standing up for so long.

—

I have to tell a second-hand story. While we were in Bagan, Sarah left us to find a clinic that could administer a rabies injection. She found one nearby but was told that the vaccine was only available at the hospital. They assured her this was a five-minute walk down the road.

Five minutes turned out to be a five-kilometre trek in the baking afternoon heat and burning sun along dusty roads to a hospital far outside town. After walking for over an hour Sarah arrived, slightly delirious, to find they spoke no English.

She mimed a dog biting her arm and an injection. They understood that part. However, Sarah also wanted an injection of immunoglobulin, which is administered via an injection into the buttcheek. Immunoglobulin can be sourced from horse blood. This was quite hard to mime. Sarah neighed like a horse and pointed at her butt. The nurse stared at her with wide eyes. Imagine the message she received: "I've been walking for hours in the dust and the heat and all I want is horse and butt. Horse and butt. Is that too much to ask?"

Needless to say, the nurse had no idea what Sarah was on about so just gave her the standard injection and sent her on her way.

The next day started with a sunrise view from one of the tallest pagodas. We set off on our scooters in the grey predawn light and found the pagoda already crowded with people awaiting the spectacle on the steep terraced flanks. We climbed to the top and chatted with a few other backpackers, waiting for the dawn.

Soon the red sun poked over the dark horizon, small and weak and shrouded by a thick haze. The silhouette of a large temple sat almost directly in front of us, and as the sun climbed towards the spire of the temple it grew in strength from red to orange to a burning yellow, until it perched on top like a great malicious eye. Strange tendrils of mist flowed in streams across the plain, just above the trees and pagodas, as if the fog was gathering itself in some distant spot to hide from the daylight.

We went separate ways for a few hours, which I spent exploring some smaller temples scattered through dusty fields, then reconvened in the afternoon at one of the larger pagodas. A large bus was there, filled with Burmese tourists. They were instantly fascinated by us and asked to take photos. A queue formed and we ended up standing there for twenty minutes while a whole busload of people took photos with us one by one.

This certainly wasn't unique to Myanmar – I was asked countless times across Asia to pose for photos. It makes me wonder what people do with these photos of strangers. Put them on the mantelpiece? Keep them in a family album?

Once the queue ended we climbed a steep and narrow staircase to the top of the pagoda to discover a breath-taking view of the plains. Hundreds of temple spires reached out of the trees towards a cloudless sky, stretching back as far as I could see to blend slowly into a hazy blue horizon. I heard Amy and Sarah gasp when they stepped out behind me.

A small boy approached. He was no more than twelve years old, carrying a brown satchel and wearing a set of patterned pink trousers.

"Hello, where you from?" he asked.

"Australia," I said.

"Wales," said Amy.

"My name is Piso. What are yours?"

We introduced ourselves. "What are you doing up here?" Sarah asked.

"No school. I'm selling postcards. But now I am tired of selling so I come up here for some peace and quiet."

"It is lovely up here," Amy said. "Do you come up here often?"

"Sometimes," Piso shrugged. "Depends. This is a very good spot. I like to come and see the paintings and buildings from the past. I also like meet people. Come, I show you the view."

He walked us around the spire and sat on the low wall separating the ledge from the drop below while we took photos.

"What do you do?" he asked, swinging his feet.

"I teach English and Amy is a musician," said Sarah.

"A teacher!" he exclaimed. "How is my English?"

"Brilliant! How did you learn it so well?"

Piso shrugged again. "We have to learn in school. I want to be a doctor. Although I am worried that I am not smart enough."

"Aw, don't say that. If you're smart enough to learn perfect English I'm sure you can become a doctor."

Silence stretched out for a moment. I took a photo of the view.

Piso jumped off the wall. "I will try!" he said. "Thank you for speaking English with me."

—

I had yet to decide what my next move would be. I had initially planned to go up to Mandalay, a city further north, but had heard mixed reviews. Sarah and Amy were heading east to Inle Lake, closer to the Thai border. They offered for me to join and so we caught an overnight bus to a lakeside town called Nyangshwe.

Once we had arrived and found a hotel we set out to find a boat that would take us out onto the lake. A long canal connects Nyangshwe to the lake itself, so we walked there and milled around next to a row of moored boats, long shallow canoes with outboard motors on the back. A man saw us and seized the opportunity. We negotiated a price and were soon putting out between banks of long grass. Birds flapped into the air at our passing. Soon the canal gave way to an expanse of shallow blue-grey water that mirrored the hazy sky above, ringed by thirsty brown hills.

Our guide putted over towards a group of fishermen

standing on the back of flat rafts with shallow edges that hovered no more than a few centimetres above the water's surface. They held nets woven around a conical frame, like a large funnel, and thrust them open-end down into the water. They then pushed a multi-pronged spear through the small end and thrust it up and down, spearing the fish trapped by the funnel. The men also had one leg curled around an oar, so they balanced on one foot, rowed with the other and used both their hands to catch fish. It was a real feat.

We putted on and entered a complex network of lush floating gardens bordered by purple flowers. Poles stuck out of the woven green mat like a forest stripped of its canopy, tended by workers in straw hats.

The guide moved us through. He was clearly familiar with the winding routes through the gardens and into a village built on stilts high above the water line. Multi-storey houses rose above the floating grass, connected by a wayward network of power lines on tilted poles. Villagers were motoring along between the houses in little canoes that shot an arc of white water into the air behind each boat.

Later that day we hired some bicycles and set off to find a cave that I'd seen on a map somewhere.

We cycled out of town towards the surrounding hills and quickly found ourselves amongst dry paddocks and scrubland. A farmer on an ancient tractor rode the other way, giving us a second glance before rolling on with a belch of black smoke. The road led over steep hill and into a small village. Small children were running towards a circle of fire burning in a field nearby, watched over by the villagers as they cleared growth from the paddocks.

I stopped to ask for directions and was sent further along the road to a small compound. It was a dead end. The sun was going down and lighting the fields nearby in an orange glow. I parked the bike and stood uncertainly.

Sarah soon arrived and leaned her bike on the kickstand. "Is this it?"

"I don't know." I lowered my voice. The buildings were quiet and seemingly lifeless.

"Do we go in?"

I nodded and walked slowly along the central path through the compound. A cat slunk out of one doorway and disappeared into another.

"Doesn't feel like there's anybody home."

Just when we turned to leave, a shoeless monk in a red robe stepped out of a doorway and smiled at us.

"Hello. We're here to see a cave?"

The man disappeared wordlessly into the dark room and reappeared a moment later with a torch. He beckoned silently for us to follow, then walked to the other side of the compound and down steep wooden steps into an opening in the ground.

We followed and stood in the darkness a moment, letting our eyes adjust. The monk swung the light around to reveal a long cavern, a few stories high and roughly the same deep. On our left, another series of steps lead down to a second cavern that was only just lit by the reflected light from the cave entrance. The right side of the cave was dark, save for where the torchlight flashed by and revealed writings on the wall or small doorways and entrances that swallowed the probing beam.

The monk walked further into the cavern, then turned to the right and descended a series of stone steps. The darkness here was now absolute. The steps ended at a small grotto and then went upwards again, this time steeper, narrower and bordered by rocks and darkness. The monk led us up, shining the light backwards to show us the way.

The steps flattened out into a narrow tunnel sloping upwards into the rock. Periodically the walls parted to reveal a small meditation chamber, a mat laid in front of a small Buddha statue, only for the darkness to swallow it whole again when the monk moved on. The statues seemed to move ever so slightly in the moment the light flicked away.

"Getting hotter," Sarah whispered behind me. The silence recoiled at the sound of her voice, then rushed back in to fill the space. The air tasted used, like breathing underneath a sheet.

The monk stopped at a fork in the tunnel and shone the light down to the right to reveal a small room. A reed mat was laid out in front of a shrine. I walked towards it but the monk beckoned me to come back.

"No oxygen," he said. It was the first time he'd spoken. He then put his hands together like a prayer, then closed his eyes and flopped his head forward before looking up with a grin.

"They meditate?" I made a prayer motion.

He nodded and flopped his head forward again.

"And they pass out?" He nodded and chuckled softly.

He pointed the torch down the left fork of the tunnel. A small ladder led upwards into another small grotto.

We poked our heads through but he wasn't willing to let us in. "Very little oxygen."

We went into the main cavern, then down to the grotto and back into the sloping tunnel. We kept our voices to a whisper. The silence still seemed alive, as if it were watching us.

"It's brilliant," Amy whispered, pushing back the quiet.

We returned to the main cavern and decided to go through a low archway. It led to another small tunnel, but this one was decorated with chalk drawings of animals and lines of script. The silence was still there, but strangely it was starting to become familiar. It was less of an invisible force, annoyed at the intrusion into its lair, and more of a comfort - almost like an old childhood blanket.

—

Sarah and Amy were heading north to Mandalay, but I was pushing on. I wanted to go to Laos before heading south to Cambodia, where I planned on staying a while to apply for onward visas. We sat playing cards in a café, waiting for the inevitable and then said a rushed goodbye when a man in a pick-up appeared to take me to the bus.

"I have a week off in a month or so," Sarah said as the guy swung my pack onto the tray. "Maybe I can come meet you somewhere. Vietnam?"

I smiled. "I'll be moving fast, but you're welcome to join. Let me know. Travelling is less fun alone."

Amy frowned. "Aw, Ewen! I want to come too! Come see me if you're ever in the UK!"

I laughed. "You don't have to say that just because I'm leaving! You can be honest."

"Ok, you're shit, never come." She grinned and gave me a hug.

I don't remember too much of the ensuing bus trip – a Slovakian guy named Peter and windy roads through steep hills. My notebook isn't helping. I think I just stared out the window and listened to quiet music.

I do remember stopping at a roadside restaurant and eating with two Americans, a young woman and an older man who was wearing glasses that made his eyes look twice their normal size.

"I'd like vegetarian noodles, but with no egg," the girl

asked the waitress. She was met by a wide-eyed look.

"No egg," she repeated. "I don't eat eggs."

"Are you vegan?" I asked.

"Oh, no, I eat cheese and milk. I just like them too much."

"So why not eggs?"

"Because, like, I'm vegetarian for moral reasons and eggs are like, future chickens."

"But only if they're fertilised," I said. "They're really just chicken periods."

The smile froze on her face and her lower jaw dropped slightly as she stared at me with a totally blank look.

"Well, like, you never know," she eventually sputtered.

The older man interjected.

"I don't like the food here. I'm not eating until we get to Thailand."

The girl nodded, relieved at the change of topic. I, on the other hand, grabbed the back of the guy's head and slammed it violently into my plate of noodles before upending the churned-up food all over the girl and storming back to the bus. Actually I didn't do that, but I did picture myself doing it. That was almost as satisfying.

5
THE PLAIN

I arrived in Chiang Mai, in northern Thailand, on a stuffy, smoggy evening. The change from Myanmar was remarkable – an almost instantaneous burst of noise, signs and minivans.

The next day I caught a tuk-tuk to Wat Umong, a large temple complex set in the jungle near the city. The trees were brown and sparse in the dry season, which left the place looking naked. The temple itself was built above a series of underground tunnels lit by intermittent skylights. A few locals prayed at shrines interspersed in the corridors but I had the place largely to myself.

I walked around the temple slowly, staying in the shade to avoid the glaring sun. A path led down to a pond that had been shrunken by the sunlight and heat. I crossed a small wooden bridge to a tiny island, no more than ten metres wide, that was occupied by huge crowd of loitering pigeons. Turtles jostled each other for space in the shrinking water. My body was too heavy to lift. I let it sit on a bench and aimed my eyes at the pond while my mind wandered. The air was hot and suffocating, even in the shade. I swatted a few insects away.

All of a sudden I decided I had no desire to stay in Thailand any longer. I wanted to move fast, to make progress home. I walked back to the hostel to book a van to Chiang Kong, on the Mekong River - the border with Laos.

The receptionist assured me no van existed. On her advice I bought a ticket to Chiang Rai, halfway to my destination, in the hope that I could find a connection there. Once I was on the van, however, I discovered that the driver was actually going all the way to the Laos border.

This sort of confusion over travel bookings was not uncommon. Whenever I boarded a train, for example, a small man would invariably spot me, waddle over and gesture for me to show him my ticket. I would oblige and he would inspect it. This inevitably attracted other small men. Once a suitable number had gathered, usually four or five, they would start arguing amongst themselves and then point at some seats before staring at the ticket again. Often this happened while I was actually sitting in the correct seat. Eventually, a taller man in uniform would intervene and seize the ticket. He would quickly discover that I was where I was supposed to be and the small men would then disperse.

A tense knot had settled in my stomach so I kept to myself during the day's drive north. We arrived at a hostel in pouring rain. The other tourists in the van were all booked to take a boat down the river and into Laos, apparently a staple on the backpacker trail, but I wanted space and some quiet.

I swung my pack onto my back and struck off towards the town centre, stopping under tin overhangs to let the squalls of rain pass over and soon found a dark, damp hotel run by an irritable fat lady.

I left my things and walked further into town. A road led down the steep riverbank to a large concrete square on the water's edge. The sun was setting, although it was hard to tell amidst the blue haze. A large stage was set up in preparation for a festival. Wafts of smoke rose from stalls selling grilled fish heads and unidentifiable meats to the locals milling about. Laos lay on the far side of the Mekong, quiet and empty. I didn't know much about Laos. I was determined to cross the river and get lost.

While I was taking a photo a man came over and tapped my shoulder.

"Come, sit, you want beer?"

"I'm alright for beer thanks, but I'll sit."

"Ok, you sit, no problem, here," He pulled up a chair next to a plastic table.

I was sharing the table with two middle-aged women holding small children. They stared at me. I smiled and said hello but they didn't move a single facial muscle in acknowledgement. The man came back and pushed a plate of unidentifiable things towards me.

"Eat, you eat, yes."

"Thanks," I reached for the plate.

I hesitated. One half of the plate contained a pile of little jellybean-shaped things, while the other half was a black mass with suspicious spindly legs poking out.

I moved my head closer for a better look while my hand remained frozen in mid-air. The black mass was a pile of grilled crickets and the jellybeans were small grubs. The breath caught in my throat and I suppressed a shiver. The man, women and children all looked at me expectantly with stone faces.

I considered my options. A tactical withdrawal, at this point, was unlikely. My hand was clearly reaching for the food, suggesting I was hungry, and that was true enough until about two seconds ago. But withdrawing the hand would insult their hospitality. I could have gone for a full-scale retreat – abruptly scrambling to my feet and sprinting away – but that would draw too much attention and I tend to suppress my own discomfort in situations like this in order to avoid a fuss. My third and final option was to eat one of the bugs, leaving me the small consolation of choosing which bug to eat.

I went for the grub. It was smaller than the crickets, which still looked like they were ready to jump off the plate. You know that scene from the Lion King, where the meerkat slurps that grub down? That is exactly what this grub looked like, except slightly smaller. It was a ridged, swollen, lumpy, sickly-yellow jellybean with tiny black legs poking out of the inside curve like a tuft of little pubic hair. I picked one up, looked at the stone faces across the table and popped it in my mouth.

I was planning on swallowing it straight down like a pill but it was dry and there was a high risk of inhalation so I reflexively chomped. A bit of liquid spurted against the inside of my cheeks. I instantly regretted that decision and swallowed quickly. The family maintained their stony gaze. One of my eyelids twitched and I swear the thing wriggled a little in my throat as it slowly descended. Even writing about it is making me queasy.

—

I crossed the river into Laos with a crowd of dreadlocked backpackers. Once everyone on our van had crossed through customs we gathered in a small café for breakfast. The woman who owned the place came out with a bottle of whisky with a dead cobra coiled inside. It stared out at us lifelessly.

"It make you man," she said, popping the lid off and offering it around.

It was nine in the morning, so far too early for alcohol, but the opportunity was unlikely to repeat itself. I took a small swig. It tasted like the inside of an antique store with no hint of cobra.

Feeling much the same about my gender as I did before breakfast, I left the others and walked across the small town to a bus stop. I was hoping to travel to a village called Luang Namtha, up near the Chinese border. I had no reason for going there in particular but it seemed quiet and out of the way.

The heat was starting to settle over the road as the sun rose higher. While I sat under the shade of the bus shelter a Laotian guy approached and sat next to me.

"Hello."

"Hello," I replied.

"My name is Vilai."

"My name is Ewen." I pushed aside my desire to be left alone and shook his hand. "How do you say your name again?"

"Vilai," he repeated, slower this time.

"Vilai. Can you teach me some Laotian? Some words? I don't know how to speak any." I took out my notebook. "How do you say hello?"

He took my notebook, thought for a moment and then wrote the word once in Laotian and again in the Roman alphabet. "Sabaidee."

"Sa-bai-dee."

He nodded and wrote again. Thank you – "kop jai."

"WhatsApp?" he asked.

I nodded, taking myself by surprise and impulsively gave him my real number.

The conversation petered on a little but his English wasn't great so we soon sat in silence.

My bus arrived shortly afterwards – an old, battered coach with peeling leather seats. A crowd gathered to pack their luggage, which included (but was not limited to) several mattresses and a live chicken in a sack. I said goodbye to Vilai and settled in with my headphones on.

Soon my neighbouring seat and the two seats behind were occupied by the only other backpackers on the bus – a French girl named Julie and a Swiss couple named Samuel and Petra. Julie was friendly at first, although her haircut looked like an open-face motorcycle helmet. She spent a lot of time talking about how great it was to be 29 and working indefinitely without pay in a hippie hostel in Thailand. Once there was a pause in her autobiography I quickly put my headphones back over my ears.

The bus chugged on for eight hours - up hills and along ridgelines, past hazy valleys and steep drops, belching black smoke with each wrenching gear change and sudden stall. My seat was stiff. Every so often the bus ground to a stop in small villages of thatched bamboo huts to offload mattresses and chickens before lurching onwards again. The jungle here was green and thick. It clogged the valleys and spread over the steep hillsides. The haze was still there, a blue shroud choking the landscape, but the green leaves were certainly an improvement on Thailand.

The four of us booked into the same hotel in Luang Namtha, which was really an abandoned construction site, and then headed to the small night market nearby for a meal. The food was great, an array of noodles and flavour, although we did encounter people eating duck eggs with an embryo inside. They're a delicacy, apparently. They smell like - well, like rotting foetus.

—

The following morning we found a store with mopeds and motorcycles for rent. Julie and I agreed to split one while Samuel and Petra took the other. While we were getting ready, Julie loudly informed us that she didn't like wearing helmets, although with her haircut I couldn't tell if her helmet was on or not anyway.

We rode north towards the Chinese border on a road that wound lazily through valleys dotted with small farms, bamboo huts and thin rivers trickling under the shade of overhanging trees. The locals all smiled and waved as we rode through small thatched villages.

After an hour or more of slow riding I changed gears around a corner and the engine whirred noisily. I pulled over. Samuel and Petra followed and we all got off to have a look.

"Uh oh," said Sam, bending down. "We cannot fix this here."

"What is the problem?" asked Julie. She removed one of her helmets.

He tapped on a metal plate near the engine. "The chain has come off on the wheel and also in the gearbox, which is behind this plate. We need some tools."

He straightened and shrugged as he put his helmet back on. "I will have to go find someone."

"We'll wait here and see if we can pull someone over," I said. "Thanks Sam."

He motored off back the way we'd come. I decided to have a look around to pass the time. We were nestled in a small, remote valley. A steep bank on the far side of the road led down to a shallow stream, where crystal clear water gurgled its way through long grass and past a tin shed rusting away amidst the green. The air was cool in the shade. There were certainly worse places to get stuck.

Sam returned with a mechanic on the back of his scooter after an hour. He'd returned to the previous village and had been roped into becoming a taxi for a number of old ladies before he found someone who could fix the bike.

The man got it up and running quickly, whereupon Julie let it be known that she was done motorcycling for the day and wished to return to Luang Namtha. We dropped her off and Sam, Petra and I continued south.

We turned off the main road and down a dirt track that followed another river into the hills. After a while we stopped in a clearing by the riverbank, next to a tiny, stilted bamboo hut with an unfinished thatch roof. The far side of the water was a green fortress of tangled vines and tall trees.

"Ewen, do you know this plant?" Sam called.

I walked over to see. He was pointing to a small green fern.

"No," I said. "What is it?"

Sam touched it and all of a sudden the whole fern folded in on itself. "It is almost alive."

"No way," I said in disbelief. I reached down to touch another and it folded over nervously. "That's brilliant."

We rode back slowly. The winding road made the low sun swing back and forth across the sky. Occasionally the road turned a corner to reveal a shack or two nestled by the riverbank, small dugout canoes pulled up into the treeline, before swinging the other way and pushing the sun back to the other side of the sky. I leaned gently on the handles, easing the motorcycle around the turns. It was quiet.

—

We were joined for dinner in the market that evening by an Irish guy named Luke. He was heading south to a town named Luang Prabang for Songkran, the Lunar New Year celebrated across Southeast Asia that is essentially the world's largest water fight. Julie decided to join us. This was disappointing news.

The van lurched off the next morning, blasting karaoke music and swerving around blind corners on the wrong side of the road as if nobody could possibly be coming the other way.

This continued for hours through toothy, jagged mountains shrouded by the omnipresent blue haze. I put my headphones on to try and drown out the wailing karaoke. It didn't work.

As the sun was going down we arrived in Luang Prabang. Songkran was already starting. Groups of teenagers had set up ambush points by the side of the road. We were soaked by buckets of water while our open tuk-tuk crawled into town. The place was alive.

Luke had been here before, so once we were dry he took us to a secluded bar located on the far side of a rickety bamboo bridge. We ordered a round and began chatting.

Julie turned to me. "See, I don't like your haircut," she said. "I don't know if you like men or women."

I stared at her and briefly entertained the image of throwing my beer in her smug, helmeted face.

"That's fine by me. It's my business who I like."

"I actually like your haircut," Luke interjected.

Julie kept talking. "Some people don't like me because I say things like that. But I just say what I think and I don't like your haircut."

I reached for my glass and held it for a moment before taking a small sip.

"See, I actually cut my hair with nail scissors," Julie continued. "I mean, hair and nails are made of the same thing, so I just cut the ends with nail scissors! It makes sense, no?" She squealed with laughter.

I resisted, with some difficulty, the obvious comeback of pointing out that the last person I'd be taking hair advice from is someone that cuts theirs into an open-face motorcycle helmet with nail scissors.

—

The next day was the first proper day of Songkran. We woke to the sound of screams and thumping music and walked outside to find a parade of pick-up trucks carrying people armed with water guns. More groups lined the roadside and the two sides were thick in battle. Each house had a hose running outside, used to refill the buckets and guns, which then pumped the water into arcs across the street. The sunlight was a burning heat and cool water was a sweet relief.

Luke and I walked down the road and joined forces with a large group of drunk locals. Initially we were both given spare water guns, but after a few minutes of ineffective fire I realised that volume of water, rather than range, was the most efficient means of making someone else wet. I found a large bucket and although it took time to fill the immense payload made it a lethal weapon.

The parade of vehicles passed slowly by, bringing continuous music and streaming water. Every so often the traffic would deliver the ultimate prize – an open tuk-tuk.

Soon Luke's cry went up. "Ewen! Tuk-Tuk! Grab the bucket!"

As I approached the tuk-tuk I saw the occupants – two passengers, presumably husband and wife. She was overweight and dressed in a full safari outfit, like she'd been reading way too much National Geographic and thought she'd spend her time in Laos riding an elephant through the jungle with local men to carry her seven suitcases full of peanut butter.

The tuk-tuk slowed to almost a complete stop. I walked calmly to the back to gain a clear shot.

"Oh my good Gawd, he's gawt a bucket!"

I planted my left foot forward and swung my torso low to get as much of my body weight behind the launch as possible. Her mouth gaped open in horror and her face froze in shock.

The water shot out in a straight, shimmering warhead that seemed to jet forward in slow motion. The woman's arms raised reflexively as the water made contact. My aim couldn't have been better. I swear I saw water spurting out of their ears.

—

I was woken early the next morning by a ding from my phone.

I squinted while my brain slowly returned to consciousness. It was a text from Vilai – "Good morning."

I stared at the screen groggily for a minute before slowly tapping out a reply. "Good morning."

After saying a brief goodbye to Luke and Julie I returned to the bus station to find a bus to Phonsavan, a town further east. Phonsavan is near the Plain of Jars, a large grassland scattered with cluster of enormous stone jars left behind by an ancient civilization. This bus took all day and the evening found me in another half-built non-descript concrete hotel with perhaps a hundred rooms and no other guests.

I say the Jars are near Phonsavan, and at the time I believed this to be true so I hired a bicycle the next morning and set off riding. Finding the Jars actually involved a difficult, uphill cycle through kilometres of bleak Laotian concrete suburbs. It was too early for Songkran revellers, so I remained dry. This was a relief at first but soon turned to a disappointment once the sweat began dripping down my face.

The suburbs eventually gave way to an open plain. After some time spent dodging speeding trucks and questioning my decisions I arrived, sweaty and tired, at a large gravel car park. A fence ringed the Plain of Jars itself, which was hidden behind a low brown rise. I locked the bike and walked towards a corrugated tin building. It was a small museum that gave some history of the Jars and of Laos.

Laos is the most heavily bombed country on Earth. During the war in neighbouring Vietnam, a Vietcong supply route known as the Ho Chi Minh trail ran through Laos and across the Plain itself. Over the course of the war the US dropped more bombs on Laos than it dropped in all of World War 2 - one planeload every eight minutes, 24 hours a day, for nine years.

I'll try and put that in perspective. If the average reading speed for an adult is 300 words per minute, that means a planeload of bombs would've been dropped on Laos in the time it has taken you to read to here from the beginning of this chapter. Now think back to where you were nine years ago. That's a lot of bombs. Many of these were anti-personnel cluster bombs. If you look up 'cluster munitions' on Wikipedia, as I just did, the example photo is actually an unexploded cluster bomb on the Plain of Jars.

I took my ticket and walked back outside to the gate to see a huge sign in English. It told me that certain paths through the plain had been cleared of unexploded ordinance, marked by white bricks. The last sentence read, 'You are advised to stay between the white markers'. Thank you for that advice, sign. I shall heed it.

I went through the gate, found some white bricks and walked between them. The white paint had faded and some bricks were covered in grass.

The first jars lay strewn at the top of a small rise. They were large rocks that had been hollowed out and lay about like stone mugs discarded by giants after a big night. The theory is that they were once burial urns, but nobody really knows for sure.

There was a large area of mown grass on the far side of the rise that was covered in hundreds of these scattered jars. Some were upright, some had fallen over and a few had been blown in half by bombs. Groups of locals were picnicking and children ran and climbed throughout the ruins. I was stopped a few times for photos but was largely left to myself. I walked through slowly, skirting the edges of huge bomb craters and admiring the scattered stone mugs littered across the plain.

—

I got back to the hotel just while the sun was going down, dropped my stuff off in my room and walked back downstairs to go and get dinner. The door back into the lobby was blocked by two backpackers, a guy and a girl. Both were facing the other way. An angry voice echoed down the concrete hallway.

I tapped the man on his back. He was huge, over a head taller than me and built like a bin lorry. He turned his head.

"Could you go and get help?" he asked in a surprisingly high and timid voice. "He's got a gun."

The girl next to him glanced at me with wide eyes.

I looked at him, at her, back at him and then past them into the lobby. A shirtless Laotian man stood blocking the exit. One arm was behind his back and he waved the other wildly. He was wearing a fedora and had a large spider, exactly like Spiderman's logo, tattooed across his chest. The hotel owner stood behind a desk on the right, worriedly twisting his hands.

"Fucking long nose!" Spiderman yelled before spotting me. "You, don't leave! Don't go! Stay there!"

I squeezed past the backpackers and into the lobby.

"Don't go," he yelled, keeping one arm behind his

back.

"I'm just going for dinner," I said, raising my hands. "Can I leave and go to eat?"

"No! Stay here, I don't have a problem with you, but don't go!"

I walked towards him slowly, palms out. Half of me was wondering if he'd pull the gun and the other half didn't believe he actually had a gun at all.

"I'm just going for dinner, ok?" I repeated. "No problem. Just going for dinner."

I was now standing in front of him, within arm's reach. I raised my hands further in a conciliatory gesture and after a tense pause, he stepped aside.

"Ok, you, no problem."

I walked past and turned to look at what he was holding behind his back. He had his hand on the butt of a small pistol tucked into the waistband of his jeans.

I walked across the road to a restaurant and asked a waitress if anyone spoke English. She pointed to a group of men and I quickly explained.

"Can you call the police?"

They looked at each other. "No, the police can't help," one said. "In this country, the police won't come. Nothing has happened. The police don't come."

I didn't understand. "They won't come? What should we do then?"

"Just go away, wait, he will go away."

Somehow this didn't seem like a good answer to take back across the road.

"Maybe you could come and talk with him?"

They agreed and we returned to the hotel lobby. Spiderman was blocking the door, hand still on his pistol, but I touched his shoulder and he let us in. The two men asked him what was going on and he let loose a tirade of swearing aimed at the two backpackers. While he was yelling and gesturing I introduced myself to the backpackers and asked what had happened.

"Erin, from Iowa," the man said, without introducing the girl. "He threw rocks at us and another guy hit her when we left their hotel so I pulled him off his motorcycle."

"They were really aggressive," the girl added. "I'm scared to think what would've happened if I was alone."

"Long nose!" yelled Spiderman. He looked at me. "Sorry, not you. Sorry for the swearing, but they're really fucking rude."

"It's ok," I smiled.

Erin and his friend started talking to the two men and the hotel owner. I wasn't sure what to do or how to help, but Spiderman didn't seem to mind me too much and getting him out of the hotel lobby seemed like a good idea. I walked up to him.

"So what did they do?" I asked.

"They fucking checked in to my hotel, then left without paying and hurt my friend."

He stuck his finger up at the Americans but kept his right hand on his gun. "Fuck you, fucking long nose, if you don't like it here, go back to your own country!" he yelled, then looked at me again. "Sorry, not you."

I put my hand on his right shoulder and gently turned him around to face the door.

"Let's go outside and chat, I think they're too scared, let them work it out."

He accepted and stepped out onto the footpath, to my relief, then turned and gestured at the Americans. I gently closed the door behind me.

"Let's walk over here."

He followed, evidently glad to have found someone that would listen to him and took his hand off his pistol.

"Sorry, they were really rude," he said loudly. "I've been to England, to France, to Australia. I have a master degree! A master degree!"

Outwardly I nodded; inwardly I doubted.

"They think they can come here, not pay for my hotel, be so rude. So rude!"

Another short, shirtless guy appeared and stood by silently, nodding in agreement. I assumed he was Spiderman's injured friend.

"Yeah, it's awful," I said. "You're right. Terrible. How could they?"

He continued his wide-eyed rant and I continued to outwardly agree with everything he said. I suspected his aggression and unnecessary flaunting of a gun was actually due to his fear of Erin, who had, after all, single-handedly lifted his friend off a moped and dropped him on the floor.

Spiderman vented for a while longer, pausing occasionally to stick his finger up at the backpackers, but calmed slowly.

I stuck my hand out. "Ok? All sorted?"

He shook. "Thank you. But they are so rude. So, so rude." He stuck his finger up at them one last time then stormed off.

I walked back inside to ask Erin and his friend if I could help them with anything. They were fine but planned on staying in their room for the night. I found dinner nearby and returned thirty minutes later to find two police officers had finally arrived and were knocking on a hotel door. The backpackers had locked themselves in, afraid that Spiderman had returned. I offered to help and knocked on the door.

"Go away please," Erin called.

"Hey, Erin? It's Ewen. What's up?"

"Oh, hey. Sorry. They're saying they're police but we're worried that guy is still out there."

"He's not, it's actually the police. They want to talk. I can hang around if you want."

"Thanks man, that'd be great. I'll be out in a sec."

He opened the door slowly, saw the police and then brought his huge frame out of the room. We sat on a nearby table with the two police officers. One took out his phone and began scrolling through Facebook as Erin explained what had happened. He had met the girl on the bus here and they had checked into Spiderman's hotel together. They found it had no running water so decided to try somewhere else, but Spiderman took issue with this and chased them on a moped driven by his shirtless friend. He tried to run the scooter into the girl, so Erin pulled him off and threw him on the ground. Spiderman then started throwing bricks so the two backpackers sought shelter in the lobby of the hotel, which is where I found them.

I left Erin talking with the police officers and walked back to my room. I checked the hallway and the courtyard below, locked the door, pulled the bed away from the window and fell into a deep sleep.

—

I left Phonsavan on a bus south, which dropped me a few hours later on a street in an unremarkable town named Paksan, somewhere in central Laos, with no means of continuing southwards.

In the absence of any other options I started walking down a major road. It was another hot day and the sun was beating down mercilessly. After a few kilometres of concrete warehouses and brown strips of overgrown asphalt I came across a bus station. I asked for buses towards a town further south but was told there were none and that I had to continue walking.

I shouldered my pack and trudged on, holding a thumb out in the hope I'd get a lift. Eventually the heat forced me into the shade of a tiny sapling. I kept my thumb out for half an hour but had no luck.

Despairing, I put my pack on again and plodded forward, staring down at my legs. They were placing one foot in front of the other with a life of their own. My back was damp with sweat and my eyes stung as I progressed deeper into the half-built concrete suburbs of this dismal Laotian town.

Eventually I found what seemed to be a bus stop – a collapsing tin roof next to a faded, lopsided sign in front of someone's house. It didn't seem the sort of place that any buses would actually stop. There was an empty café across the road. I crossed and dropped my pack. The owner appeared and looked at me warily.

"Sabaidee," I said, picking up a menu off the table. It had no pictures so I smiled and pointed at a random word.

"This?" I asked hopefully.

She maintained a confused look. I was probably pointing at the word for 'price' or 'main meals' or something.

I mimed eating with chopsticks. This had no effect.

I pointed at something else. "This? Eat? Kop jai."

This worked. She leapt into action and I was soon provided with a hot soup. This wasn't exactly what I'd been hoping for (I'd been sweating hot soup for hours) but it was nice to eat and to sit for a while. I decided to wait there just in case some divine intervention occurred and a bus actually pulled up at this stop.

Unbelievably, one actually did. I couldn't believe my luck and got on without caring where it was going. There were two other backpackers on board, an Italian named Matteo and a British guy named Haran. We quickly struck up a conversation and agreed to find a hotel room together in the next major town.

My phone buzzed while I drifted off to sleep that night. It was Vilai. "Goodnight."

—

After a breakdown and a change of buses we arrived in Thakek, a town in southern Laos. It was close to a well-known scenic road so we hired mopeds the next morning and set off east towards the mountains that run down central Laos. The ever-present blue haze sat low, shrouding the horizon. The heat from the sun made the black leather seat on my moped hot to touch.

Soon we saw a sign for a cave called Xieng Liap that pointed down a dirt track. This ran for a short time before ending in a grove of trees. We left the mopeds there and followed a narrow but well-trodden path through the undergrowth to a small, dark scar at the base of a cliff. Matteo entered first, lighting the way with his phone.

Soon the rock walls narrowed and turned a corner, instantly removing all light from the outside. A thin cleft wound deeper into the mountain. We followed slowly using only a weak light until the cleft gave way to an enormous cavern that was lit by an arching entrance on its far side.

This was a cathedral carved from rock, dwarfing the river inside that streamed from somewhere under the earth. The water formed black pools that themselves were overlooked by enormous boulders, but the ceiling remained distant even from these. Stalactites hung from above, as if the mountain itself was trying to reach down and touch the floor.

We split up to walk around the cave, keeping quiet to avoid disturbing the brooding silence that was broken only by the trickling stream. The cave bent around again to reveal a third entrance, larger than the others, an archway over a still pool that stretched from the darkness out into the sunlight.

I found a ledge on the side and sat a while as the others explored. My back was resting against a stalagmite that was almost touching a stalactite above. Against my better judgement, I impulsively scratched a tiny 'E' into the stalagmite with a little pebble. The rock was soft, almost like cheddar.

We left the cave using the large entrance and motored further into the dry, brown mountains. They were jagged and steep, like dragon's teeth lodged in the green paddies below.

Eventually the time came for me to turn around. Matteo and Haran were intending to complete a three-day loop on the mopeds, but I intended to push on towards Cambodia the next day. We said goodbye at the side of the road and I returned the way we'd come. The way back felt significantly faster, as return journeys usually do.

The next morning I caught a bus to Phnom Penh, a journey that didn't end until late at night. There I met a friend of mine named Mat. He and his girlfriend Hannah had kindly offered me a place to stay while I applied for Chinese and Russian visas. A break from the road was welcome and so was the promise of a daily warm shower, food and time spent being immobile. I put my pack down in their kitchen and didn't pick it up again for ten days.

6
The Jungle

My days in Phnom Penh were slow and relaxed. Mat and Hannah live in a nice apartment, but it was unfortunately close to a loud karaoke bar. This meant that while I lay on the couch every night a middle-aged Chinese businessman sang me softly to sleep with a voice that sounded like he was also having a colonoscopy.

Mat showed me some of the sights around the city - a local market that sold everything from live, squirming fish to clothing and musical instruments, as well as some of his favourite restaurants and pubs. I dropped my passport off with a travel agent to get a visa for China and began preparing the paperwork I'd need to apply at the Russian embassy the following week.

One afternoon I visited S21, also known as Tuol Sleng. This was once a notorious prison set up in an old school by the Khmer Rouge, the Communist dictatorship that carried out a genocide in Cambodia in the 1970s. It was set amidst a dense cityscape of liquor stores and restaurants. There was little to indicate from the outside what it used to be except for a wall crowned by coiled barbed wire.

I bought a ticket and walked into a large courtyard flanked on two sides by imposing concrete buildings. Each level was composed of doorways that opened onto open-air hallways overlooking the courtyard. The graves of the last fourteen prisoners killed by the guards just before liberation sat in the centre of the yard, the only visible change to what it must have looked like during the time of the Khmer Rouge. Rows of palm trees swayed ever so slightly in a breeze I couldn't feel. The air at ground level was baked into place by the sun.

I'd rented an audio guide, which led me into the first building on my left. The horror hit hard and fast. These rooms were used for torture and had been left exactly as they'd been found. Metal bed frames stood in the centre of old classrooms with walls of peeling concrete, floors of faded chequered tiles and barred windows. Ammunition tins and metal rods lay on some of the cots. Each room had a photo mounted on the wall of what it looked like when Vietnamese soldiers liberated the prison. Bodies lay on each metal frame, their disfigured heads sitting in pools of blood. There were still discolorations on some of the tiles – dark brown drops splashed across the floor.

The next building was where the prisoners were kept in between interrogations. Hastily erected brick walls divided these classrooms into shower-sized cubicles. Bloodstains were visible on the walls and floor. I walked slowly through in stunned silence, listening intently to the audio guide.

The atrocities committed here could occupy a whole book. One building contained skulls found with pickaxe wounds, which were used to save bullets. Another displayed the photos of everyone known to have died here. Of the 20,000 people who entered, only fourteen survived. It was a confronting, moving place – absolutely worth a visit, but don't count on being able to do much with the rest of your day. It takes a heavy toll.

—

The Russian consulate was only open on Mondays and Thursdays, so I had a weekend to stop bumming around and go to Angkor Wat. I caught an all-day bus to the nearby city of Siam Reap and found an empty hotel.

Angkor Wat itself is actually a few kilometres from Siam Reap. It is part of the ancient city of Angkor, which once occupied an area of land larger than modern-day Paris and was centred on the large temples at its core. The temples are all that remain: Angkor Wat is the largest (and is also the largest religious monument in the world), but it is surrounded by a multitude of other temples that together make for several weeks' worth of sightseeing. I only had one day, but I didn't mind. I was slightly templed-out after two months in Southeast Asia.

The tuk-tuk driver dropped me at the entrance to Angkor Wat. A long stone causeway led over the moat to the temple itself, which was guarded by an imposing wall. Beyond was an enormous brown grass field with a central path running towards the distant temple. The stones shimmered in the sunlight. It was a long approach in oppressive heat and by the time I'd finally reach the foot of Angkor Wat I was dreaming of jumping into the moat outside.

The temple itself was an intricate network of frescoed hallways and carved columns surrounding small courtyards. The complex tapered slowly upwards in a labyrinth of stone towards a central spire. I followed the main path upwards, winding through the throngs of people trying to find an unoccupied corner for a photo. The temple sheltered me from the sun, but it still made itself known through the heat that radiated off every stone and in every gust of hot wind that blew down dark corridors.

A few people were exploring around me but the majority were in a long snaking queue to climb into the final terrace. The size of the place made it easy to find somewhere in the shade away from the rush. I sat and sipped at a water bottle.

Despite its size, I just couldn't push myself to appreciate Angkor Wat. It suffers from the weight of expectation. It may be the world's largest religious monument, but it is so sprawled that this feels like a technicality. Most of the area within the moat is brown grass and trees. I sat a while before beginning the long trek out underneath an angry sun.

From Angkor Wat I caught a tuk-tuk to Ta Prohm, another stone temple hidden in the trees. This was where they filmed one of the Tomb Raider movies. It's in the process of being swallowed by the jungle – a crumbling ruin covered in muscular trees that are slowly breaking the stones apart with enormous roots, like a terrestrial Atlantis being ripped apart by giant squid. Mounds of fallen masonry littered small courtyards flanked by teetering moss-lined columns. This was Cambodia as you'd imagine – collapsing stone doors framed by tree roots, dark recesses blocked by fallen stone, carved faces gazing out from underneath the encroaching forest.

—

I returned to Phnom Penh to apply for a Russian visa. I expected this to be an arduous process. Russians, you see, love bureaucracy and hate tourists - a disastrous combination when you're a tourist in search of a visa. The application that I'd printed and filled out before going to the embassy was so detailed that I half-expected to be asked for a sample of pubic hair.

My phone buzzed early on a Monday morning and roused me from sleep. It was Vilai, of course. "Good morning."

I arrived at the Russian embassy when it opened. The place was massive, set on a square kilometre of land and surrounded by a long concrete wall topped with razor wire. It reminded me of an old-fashioned mental asylum.

I rang a doorbell on the wall. A small door clicked open into a small fenced courtyard, watched by security cameras. A few other people were milling around.

After a while a large man with spiky hair emerged from a door. He looked the offspring of a bear and a hedgehog. He watched us for a moment then summoned a woman with his pointer finger. She disappeared through the doors.

After another quarter hour or so Hedgehog appeared again to summon another. People were selected like this for an hour and a half before my turn eventually came.

I followed Hedgehog inside. He spoke to me in Russian and gestured at a drawer.

"Phone."

I put it in the drawer then went through a metal detector and sat down in a small room to await my fate.

A woman soon entered and asked for my paperwork. She took one glance at it and gave it back.

"Wrong form."

"But I printed all these off your website," I replied incredulously.

"I sorry. Wrong form. Go this website. Fill in form. Print double sided. Come back."

"Can you print out a copy for me to fill in here?"

"No. Go internet café."

She turned and left. I looked at Hedgehog for help but he just stared at me impassively from eyes set deep in his face.

I left in despair. It was almost ten in the morning and the consular section closed at twelve. I went to find an Internet café with a printer but instead found a printing shop with no Internet followed shortly by an Internet café with no printers. It was shaping up to be one of those days.

I returned to Mat and Hannah's, filled in the form, took a USB to a printing shop, printed the form according to specific instructions detailing the page width and other bollocks before returning to the embassy an hour later, flustered and sweaty.

I sat in the courtyard and felt something tickling my upper arm. I looked down and saw a small ant. I flicked it off. My neck tickled. I swatted it quickly then looked at my hand. Another small ant. I swore silently.

Hedgehog summoned me again. I rubbed my face and neck vigorously to squash any wayward ants before following him inside.

The same woman took my paperwork and after examining it over for almost an hour she re-emerged and took my passport and money. I took this to mean that I'd get a visa. I smiled to myself when I left. The way was clear.

I waited a few more days enjoying nightly lullabies from my colonically-challenged Chinese businessman. Soon the time came to leave. I said a reluctant goodbye to Mat and Hannah and shouldered my pack again. It was heavy and suddenly I was wrenched back to the road on a bus towards Vietnam.

I wasn't alone for long. Not long I stepped off the bus in the centre of Ho Chi Minh City, I sat on a bench to get my bearings and was approached by two young Vietnamese, a guy and a girl.

"Hello, what is your name?" the guy asked, extending his hand.

I looked up and saw them smiling down at me.

"Uh, Ewen," I said, shaking his hand.

"Uh-Ewen," he repeated.

"No, sorry. Just Ewen."

"Hi Just Ewen. I am Max."

"Hi Max, nice to meet you." I stood up and faced the

girl. "What is your name?"

"An," she replied. "We would like to practice English, if that is ok."

"Have you just arrived?" asked Max.

"Five minutes ago. I'm looking for a place to stay."

He nodded knowingly. "There's a good place, not far from here. I don't have time to walk you there, but maybe you have a map?"

I nodded and opened my phone. He pointed to a place a few blocks away.

"It's pretty good, the city is busy but maybe they have some space. It's just down that road."

I thanked him. The conversation flowed for a few minutes – what I was doing, where I'd been. They were both students, although An also worked in a hotel and was on her lunch break, so they soon had to leave. I was meeting Sarah later, whom I'd met in Myanmar, so I asked if they wanted to go for a coffee the next day to practice English with us. They smiled and agreed.

I met Sarah that evening and we found the hostel Max told me about – a decent, small place. We spent the next morning wandering around the city. The heat was oppressive, a constant force that pushed us towards the shade of trees as we slowly walked the streets.

We met Max and An that afternoon in a café he'd chosen, a niche artisan place with people studying and all conversation kept to a low murmur. The conversation flew easily. Soon, however, I noticed that Max was no longer making eye contact with me at all. An remained quiet. Shortly afterwards she received a phone call, stepped outside and returned with two middle-aged businessmen.

Sarah and I exchanged glances. The smile seemed

frozen on Max's face and he still wasn't meeting my eye. I shifted my weight forward in the chair.

The businessmen sat down and introduced themselves. They were on assignment from South Korea and turned out to be fast talkers so the conversation quickly resumed. Max, meanwhile, had relaxed again and was soon throwing jokes my way although they seemed less like casual banter and slightly more pointed.

While An and I were speaking with the businessmen Max stood up and walked outside. After a short pause, Sarah glanced at her phone and followed him. They both returned shortly afterwards but didn't sit down.

"I think we should go," Max said.

Sarah took the lead. "It was nice to meet you!" she said to the businessmen, who seemed taken by surprise. An stood up quickly and I took the cue.

"It was great!" I said, then followed Sarah, Max and An outside.

"I'm so confused. What was that all about?" I asked.

Sarah laughed. "So those two guys are actually staying at An's hotel and must have got her number from another receptionist. They essentially followed her to that café."

"Ah," I said. "Well that's bizarre."

After dinner Max and An took us to a karaoke bar, which seemed like a cruel joke after Phnom Penh. The place turned out to be less of a bar and more of a hotel. Every group was given an individual room with leather couches arranged around a small TV and two microphones. Conversation was basically impossible so we all sat there drinking beer after beer while our eardrums were audibly beaten to death by whoever was currently squawking for three to four minutes. I can't say it was the best way I've ever spent an evening, but it wasn't totally terrible.

—

From Ho Chi Minh City we caught an overnight bus to a picturesque little town called Hoi An. On the bus, we met a young bearded English guy named Hayden, who agreed to come with us to find a hotel.

The streets of Hoi An were small, lined with terraced houses and strung with the familiar tangle of power lines. A man on a moped pulled up beside us as we walked.

"Hotel? Hotel?" he asked.

Sarah looked at me. "Maybe we should give it a go."

"Maybe. What do you think, Hayden?"

He shrugged. "Could be alright. I'm a bit tired of walking."

"Just across bridge," the man said excitedly, pointing across the river. "Very close, not far!"

We collectively shrugged and followed him to a palatial hotel complex on the opposite bank. There were no other guests in sight.

"Seems nice," said Hayden.

I looked around. How do places like this stay open?

We dropped our stuff off and wandered through Hoi An. It was busy, but in an almost ordered, quiet way. Narrow, tree-lined streets wound this way and that, overhung by lanterns and flanked by single-story yellow terraces and tiled rooftops hidden amongst flowers and dense foliage. It was a welcome change from the hustle, as if we'd drifted into a sheltered eddy hidden amidst a fast-flowing river.

We stopped at a market stall for a coffee and something to eat. The lady turned to Sarah.

"Your hair, so nice! So so nice! May I touch?"

"Sure!"

She began to braid Sarah's hair. Hayden and I chuckled, but it soon became clear that the braiding was going to take some time so we abandoned Sarah to her unexpected appointment and wandered slowly through the streets and alleys, across covered stone bridges, in and out of temples.

Some of the old yellow houses, once homes to wealthy merchants, were now museums open to the public. We found one and entered. It was still. The interior rooms were built around a central courtyard, itself lined by balconies on three sides and a stone wall on the fourth. A fountain trickled in the centre. The house was supported by enormous timber beams that shut out all outside sound, leaving only the fountain and the squeaks of floorboards as we walked curiously through.

Asia is a hectic place – loud, busy, bustling, moving, talking, smiling, driving, a rapid stream of sound and movement. My schedule was the same. I had set myself a large distance to traverse and I was budgeting time for crossing Mongolia and Russia. This meant I had to move fast, never staying more than a few nights in any spot. I only had a day in Hoi An, but it was a moment to breathe. I took my time moving through each room in the ancient house, savouring each display cabinet, enjoying the sound of creaking floors.

"Good morning." Vilai again.

I wrote back another "good morning." He didn't respond.

Once the others were ready we hoisted our backpacks and walked back across the river to the local bus stop, where Sarah and I said goodbye to Hayden. We were heading to Hanoi, which involved a day of being shuttled from one bus to another.

The road took us along the coast, skirting steep hills on

one side and the ocean on the other. We were seated right at the back of the bus with a German guy named Luca. There was a strong smell coming from the toilet.

Luca told us that he was riding a moped across Vietnam. This lead to the obvious question about why he was on the Poo-mobile and where his moped was.

"Ah, I'm getting a bit sick of it. Honestly, my arse really hurts. It kinda sucks, riding a moped all day."

"What did you do with the moped?"

"Oh, I've still got it. It's underneath, with all the bags in the luggage compartment."

At this point the bus suddenly stopped. This wasn't unusual – it had been periodically stopping and on a few occasions had actually reversed back down the motorway for a few minutes before changing gears and driving forward again.

On that note, this happened on almost every bus I took in Asia and was a reoccurring mystery. Sometimes the bus would stop to pick people up, which made sense. Sometimes the bus would stop to unload and load boxes. That also made sense. Sometimes, however, the bus stopped for no reason at all and even reversed for minutes at a time. What reason could there be to reverse a coach back down a dual carriageway? A true riddle.

This brings me to a few other mysterious observations I made and would like to mention here. I often saw people standing outside their houses and watering the road with a hose. Not cleaning the road, mind you, but standing dreamily and watering the asphalt like you'd water a plant. Also, local men had a habit of lifting their shirts up to show their bellies. Sometimes we'd drive past groups of men standing and talking to each other while they scratched their large hairy bellybuttons. Does it give relief from the heat? It is a show of manhood? I do not know.

The driver stopped reversing down the motorway and asked us all to vacate the coach, so we stood by the side of the road in small groups. Liquid was leaking out the back of the bus. The driver and a gathering of small men who had appeared out of nowhere peered inside and quickly set to work removing large metal objects from the coach's innards.

A pair of tourists, a mother and her son, stood by the bus door waiting silently and intently for the repairs to finish. The son had an amazingly upright posture. He looked like a human erection.

Eventually we learned that the toilet system had sprung a leak. They had patched it but not cleaned it. I spent the rest of the ride in a pungent state of semi-consciousness.

The Portaloo arrived in Hanoi the following morning. We stepped out into a cacophony of car horns and an endless swirl of mopeds, rivers of them flowing past large green parks, before walking to the old city to find somewhere to stay. I left Sarah to try to arrange a Mongolian visa, an unsuccessful endeavour that only resulted in being ripped off by a taxi driver with a 'faulty' meter.

That evening Sarah and I met up with a friend of hers named Dan, who was teaching English in Hanoi. He took us to a quiet bar built over railway tracks that were walled-in by tall, densely packed buildings. People used the tracks as a thoroughfare and moved aside only for the trains, which slid past our window with only centimetres to spare. Each time one clacked past and rattled the room with a roar, everyone in the bar clinked their glasses together and downed the contents before continuing our separate conversations.

Sarah and I said a sad goodbye afterwards. She was heading back to Bangkok and I was pushing on to the next chapter of this trip – China. After she caught her bus and disappeared in the swirl of traffic I sat in a café on a street corner in the old town, near the arch of an ancient city gate and watched Hanoi flow past. I had rushed through southeast Asia almost as fast as it was rushing past me now while I sat, quietly sipping on a green tea, thinking of the people whose lives had briefly intersected with mine before we all stepped back into the hustling crowds.

I thought back to stepping off the cruise ship in Singapore, walking through towering steel-lattice trees in the Gardens by the Bay; to Max, Maisie, the heat of Malaysia, the jungle walks and the street art of Georgetown; to the hostel in Bangkok, being treated to dinner on my birthday by a group of people I'd met only two hours before; to Myanmar, the slow, wobbly train pushing through the encroaching foliage, meeting Sarah and Amy, the endless plains of Bagan and the dark, forbidden cave watched by the silent monk; Laos, cathedral caverns and dragon-back mountains; Cambodia, dinners with Mat and Hannah, crumbling ruins and monstrous trees; and to Vietnam, loud streets and flowing mopeds.

There was a buzz in the air here and it wasn't just the din of horns and the drone of small motorbikes. It was a drive, an engine rumbling underneath it all that had picked me up and, for a short while, taken me along.

7
THE CITIES

I left Hanoi on an overnight train towards Nanning, China. I was staying in a cabin with two Chinese girls, both English speakers, who were on their way home from a holiday in Vietnam. They quickly struck up a conversation and taught me some crucial Chinese phrases like "Hello. Train? Train station. Thank you." We drew the attention of others in the carriage and soon a large number of people were having an animated debate in Chinese about the best way to get me to Guangzhou.

On the collective advice of everyone on board I changed trains in Nanning, an anonymous concrete city that was my first taste of China. The first thing I noticed stepping out onto the street was the sudden silence. There were no horns, no rush of mopeds - just normal traffic sticking to well-defined road rules and stopping at functional traffic lights.

The second thing I noticed was that I was, for the first time, functionally illiterate. In southeast Asia most languages used familiar letters so I could at least read city names at bus stops or train stations. Here I couldn't read a thing. I stared at Chinese characters that seemed to depict a book in a microwave or a person swallowing a computer.

The girls had written 'Guangzhou' in my notebook, which I showed to a passer-by. She walked me to the ticket hall and put me in the right queue. I then showed my 'Guangzhou' sign to the man at the ticket counter. And so, through the help of assorted strangers, I found myself on a bullet train shooting across a green landscape of rice paddies and jagged hills at two hundred kilometres an hour. It was a nice change from reversing slowly down a motorway.

I was meeting a school friend in Guangzhou named Tim, who had been living there for a few months teaching English. I disembarked at Guangzhou South, the most enormous train station I've ever seen in my life. Acres and acres of polished concrete were covered by a glass canopy.

I soon saw Tim's lanky frame lumbering in my direction, towering over everyone around him. "Tim! Mate, good to see you," I said, giving him a hug. My eyes were level with his nipples.

"Ewen! Jesus, your face! What is that thing?"

I scratched my beard. "This? It's for warmth."

"You'll get plenty of attention with it here!"

It was a relief to see Tim. He was a familiar face in an unfamiliar country and I was more than happy to let someone else lead the way. He hailed a taxi outside and we started driving towards his apartment.

I was under the impression that Guangzhou South was somewhere in the city centre itself, like King's Cross or Grand Central Station, so as the taxi pulled off I looked up at what I believed were the skyscrapers of central Guangzhou.

"How far are we from your place?"

"Ages away yet. These are the suburbs."

"This isn't Guangzhou?"

"Well it is, but we're on the outskirts. Maybe twenty kilometres from the city centre."

I looked out the window again. We were driving on a huge motorway past towering apartment buildings and high-rise office blocks. It felt for all the world like the centre of a big city, but these were distant suburbs.

The scale of everything was my third and lasting impression of China. It is hard to put into words because there is no equivalent that I can compare it to. Everything is just, well, absolutely massive. The station was massive, the highway was massive, the buildings were massive, the city was massive. We drove for 45 minutes, at motorway speeds, through buildings that wouldn't look out of place in centre-city New York. It was a powerful first impression.

Eventually we arrived at Tim's apartment, located on the 50-somethingth floor of an apartment complex surrounded by innumerable other 70-story buildings. I dropped my pack, had a shower and we went for a walk.

We chatted and caught up while we walked past glass monoliths and under pedestrian overpasses, down clean, ordered streets populated by electric buses and quiet cars. Buildings towered over us, stretching as far as I could see.

"So what's it like, living here? Enjoying it?"

"Yeah, loving it. But it's different," said Tim.

"Yeah? Culture, scale, language?"

"Everything. Almost nothing is the same."

"What was a stand-out, 'how did my life lead me here' moment?"

Tim thought for a moment as a bus quietly slid past. It had friendly-looking cartoon characters plastered on the side. Nearby, a group of teenagers were playing basketball at a new sports complex.

"So, a few weeks ago my school went on an excursion. I teach young kids, right, like eight to twelve years old. The school wanted them to organise the trip."

"Wanted the kids to organise it?"

"Yeah. As in, they choose the destination and how we get there. The idea was to get them to learn how to cope with some independence and to learn from any mistakes that they make when planning the day out."

"Sounds risky. So the teachers just go with whatever

the kids plan?"

"Yeah. No input. I brought up my concerns with the head teacher, but she just said don't worry, it'll be fine, it's good for them. In fact I brought it up multiple times but I kept getting shut down."

"So how'd it turn out?"

"Well, the kids decided that it would be better to save money by walking instead of catching the bus. The trouble was, there was no way to walk to where we were going, so the kids planned on walking down the side of the motorway."

"What? Surely they would intervene?"

"Nope. I kept telling the head teacher that this was the worst idea I'd ever heard and even threatened to quit over it, but they insisted. So, in the end I found myself walking alongside forty Chinese children down the shoulder of a motorway to go and visit a museum."

I couldn't help but laugh. "Tim, that's insane."

"Tell me about it. I was shitting myself the entire time. Everyone was ok in the end, thank god, but it was one of the most stressful mornings of my life."

That evening we went for a drink with his flatmates and some other expats living in the city. The night started well. We were sitting upstairs at a popular bar and various people came and went.

The conversation soon turned towards what it is like to live in China. Tim's flatmate A.J was particularly vocal.

"Ugh, I get sick of it man. The queue-jumping especially. It's the everyday things here that you just never get used to."

Some others nodded in sympathy.

"They're just different here. People don't change. And they come to England and don't change either."

Tim, normally a quiet guy, turned to face him. "A.J, that makes no sense. How much effort have you made? Do you even speak any Mandarin?"

"No, but that's not the same really, is it?" A.J. retorted. "Nothing against the Chinese personally, but it's different when people come to the UK. People can't just come over however they like and not adopt English culture or try to be a part of England. I don't want to go home to children shitting in bins."

"A.J, you're an immigrant. We're all immigrants."

A.J. just shrugged. "Yeah, but like I said, that's different."

Frustrated, Tim ignored this and turned to face me while A.J continued the conversation with a Pakistani man sitting next to him.

"I don't get it, you know? So many of these guys need China for their career, they came here because they couldn't get a job at home, make no effort to learn the language or anything and are still anti-immigrants. How can they be so close-minded?"

I shrugged. "I don't get it either. But he probably won't change his mind."

Tim paused. "It can be frustrating here, I get that. Some people do let their kids shit in bins. I'm here for less than a year, so it's fine for me, but A.J. is stuck. He lives here because he has no choice."

"Would you stay?"

Tim thought for a moment. "No. I wouldn't want to teach English forever."

Suddenly A.J. and the Pakistani guy he was speaking to stood up and started swearing at each other.

"You racist!" the man screamed. "Racist! Fucking American!"

"I'm not a fucking American!" A.J. yelled back.

The Pakistani guy stripped his shirt off and began walking around the bar, screaming at A.J. to come and fight him. The rest of us took this as our cue to leave, but when we were on the way out the Pakistani man rushed at A.J with his chest puffed out. I was unfortunately in the way and caught unawares. A woman next to me caught his arm. It was then that I was suddenly hit by an overwhelming sense of unreality. Here I was, in a city in southern China, holding on to a Pakistani man's warm, naked torso at three in the morning. What series of decisions led me here?

I let go as security rushed over and caught up with Tim to head home.

—

The sheer size of China presented me with a tough decision. I'd need at least two months to even scratch the surface of the country. This was a lot of time on my increasingly limited budget. I also needed to apply for a Mongolian visa in Beijing, which could take a week, and Mongolia was the main reason I had chosen this route. My options were to either spend not enough time in China and not enough time in Mongolia, or no time in China and enough time in Mongolia.

I decided on the latter and caught an overnight train from Guangzhou straight up to Beijing, moving at a constant 120 kilometres per hour. I spent most of this time staring out the window, first at lakes with sharp, cloud-shrouded mountains rising out of the water like the spines of sleeping dragons and then at endless rice paddies underneath gigantic concrete motorway overpasses that cut across the countryside. I also spent a bit of time pondering why my fellow passengers felt the need to constantly lubricate the floor with their saliva. My beard succeeded in making a fascinated child walk straight into a door.

I had stepped on to the train on a humid evening and almost twenty-four hours later I stepped out into a chilly spring afternoon 2000 kilometres away. My breath was visible in the air. This, I was surprised to learn, was the slow train. The fast train does the same distance in ten hours.

I decided to head straight to the Mongolian embassy. As I'd learnt in Bangkok, embassies are often closed and visa applications take time.

I emerged from the subway station onto a street that was six lanes wide and lined with imposing buildings that seemed to occupy a cubic kilometre each. While I stood there, blinking and orientating myself, a young guy approached.

"Hi! English?"

"Yes," I replied, looking at him. He was smartly-dressed. Designer stubble peppered his chin.

"Can I help you? You are lost? Looking for somewhere?"

"I'm actually looking for the Mongolian embassy." I pulled some crumpled paper from my pocket. "This is the address."

He looked at it for a moment. "Ah yes, not far. If you like, I can show you. I have just finished my class in English over there, so if you don't mind we can speak and I can practice."

"Sure," I said and smiled back. "Thanks! What is your name?"

"Rock."

"Rock? Like a pebble?"

"Yes, Rock, like rocks," he replied. "This way!"

Rock walked off and I scrambled to follow. He led me through car parks, down side roads and into a leafy embassy neighbourhood filled with stately mansions, imposing security fences, guards and fluttering flags. We soon found the Mongolian embassy. A small hut for visa applications was built into the compound wall. It was closed. Typical.

"Ah," Rock said. "Not open until tomorrow. What do you do now?"

I sighed. "I should find somewhere to stay, I suppose."

"Do you know where?"

"Not yet."

He clapped my shoulder. "Do not worry. If you like, I have some time. I can show you somewhere to stay. The best places near Tiananmen Square, only a few stops."

I let Rock lead the way back to the subway as clouds rolled in overhead. Sure enough, he rode with me to Qianmen, near Tiananmen Square, talking all the way. We walked into a neighbourhood of low stone buildings in a light, drizzling rain and found a hostel. It was fully booked. He helped me find another, translated and once the room was sorted he extended his hand again.

"Good! This is good place for you! Nice neighbourhood, lots of food."

"Thanks so much Rock!" I said, shaking his hand. He had taken over two hours out of his day and gone far out of his way.

"No problem, no problem. Help anytime!"

He walked off towards the subway. I set off to find dinner with high spirits in spite of the damp and moody sky.

—

Beijing is an interesting city. It is not like Kuala Lumpur, Bangkok or Guangzhou, fast-paced and full of skyscrapers and monorails. It is stately, immense and grand, more of a Washington DC than a New York. It also contrasts.

The neighbourhood I was staying in is known as a *hutong*, a network of narrow alleyways running between old, cramped single-story stone houses with grey tiled rooftops. The alleys ran this way and that underneath swinging shop signs, occasionally opening to reveal indoor food courts ringed by loud sizzling woks before closing in again and running past dark, hushed bars and quiet doors, all shut to the rain. I found dinner in a brightly-lit courtyard and sat a while, reading my book and writing notes in my journal.

I returned to the embassy the following morning to fill out paperwork. It would take a week and so I had a few days to see Beijing and a weekend to venture out to the Great Wall.

I made my way back to Tiananmen Square to visit the Forbidden City, something I had long been looking forward to seeing. While I was in line for security to leave the subway I heard someone calling out. It was a young guy on the other side of the barrier. He was talking to me.

"Hey! Hello! How are you?"

"Good thanks," I replied hesitantly.

"Where are you from?"

"Australia."

"Oh good! I would like to practice my English, if that's ok," he said. "I am here with my friend and we are learning English."

I smiled. "No problem. I'm going to the Forbidden City if you want to walk with me."

"Maybe we could go for a coffee?" he asked. "And talk for a little bit."

A few thoughts ran through my head. The first was that I needed a coffee. As he went off to find his friend and I went through security, my second thought was that something wasn't right. It was a gut feeling, fleeting but palpable. I thought of

Rock and how we'd met in exactly the same circumstances. Maybe I was being too judgemental.

He met me with his friend once I passed through security, a woman roughly my age and they both introduced themselves.

We left the subway station, chatting away. They asked about what I was doing, I asked what they were doing and they were vague with the details – something about looking to practice English in their spare time. This was plausible. I had been approached multiple times by people genuinely looking to practice their English; Max and An in Ho Chi Minh City, a man in Hanoi, Rock just the day before. The woman walked ahead and made a phone call.

She quickly selected a cafe and asked if it was ok. The door did say 'Coffee and Tea' on it, as you'd expect at a café, so I agreed and we went in. Nobody else was inside.

At this point you're probably wondering why I wasn't cottoning on to the fact that I was getting scammed. Well, to tell you the truth, I'm wondering exactly the same thing. I kept making excuses for all the red flags. She was on the phone to her friends and maybe the coffee shop wasn't busy that day. In my mind, the only way they'd get my money would be if some huge dude stepped out from behind a corner and robbed me blind. As there was no huge dude in sight I decided nothing could go wrong.

We sat down and a waitress brought drinks quickly along with plates of biscuits and crackers. The conversation flowed well enough. The woman said she was a nurse from near Shanghai and the guy was learning English full time. The coffee was real.

At one point the guy asked me if I liked red wine.

"Sure," I replied, wondering what he was on about.

"Maybe we should drink some red wine? After all, red is the colour of the Chinese flag and you are in China."

This struck me as an odd thing to say, but I made an excuse for him. He was just being friendly. Maybe he was trying to relate to me. I turned down the wine. There were more red flags here than in a Soviet military parade but all the warnings were echoing around the dusty, cavernous interior of my skull.

All of a sudden they decided they had to leave. I was already in the habit of putting red flags in one ear and pulling them straight out the other so I didn't think much of this either. Then the bill came. It was for something close to $120.

I was stunned. The guy and girl seemed surprised but not shocked. I went through the bill and every item was accounted for with a price next to it. My coffee cost $8, the biscuits cost $30 for each tray and the tea made up the rest. The cogs of my brain were whirring at full speed, making a sound akin to a small moped red-lining down a motorway.

"Is this normal?"

He shrugged. "This is a touristy area, it's expensive but not too surprising. We'll split it, don't worry."

There was nothing to do but pay up, so we did and went outside. I was sullen, understandably so after parting with $40 for a coffee and was preoccupied with justifying it in my head. These thoughts ranged from denial ($40 isn't much in the grand scheme of things), to resignation (no point letting it bother you), to sentiment (you can't put a price on friendship).

"Are you ok?" the woman asked.

"It was a lot of money."

"Yeah," she agreed. "But it was good to get to know you."

'There,' I thought to myself. 'Can't put a price on that, can you?'

The guy then checked the time and said they had to go meet their friends. It was after they walked away that finally, after sailing like Voyager 1 through the dark void inside my cranium, that the thought I might have been ripped off finally collided with some neurons.

I walked back to the café and found it dark and closed. I banged on the door. The waitress came out from a hallway and stared at me. I banged again, harder this time. She came, opened the door and wordlessly handed me back my money.

Satisfied, I turned away and pondered my next move. Part of me wondered what would happen if I bumped into the guy and the girl again. I checked the time. I had nothing planned for the day other than the Forbidden City. So, buoyed by my success in recovering my money, partly because I was feeling confrontational and also partly out of curiosity, I decided to go back to the subway station and play the fool.

As I was walking back a local called out to me. "Hi, speak English? I practice? Maybe we go for a drink?"

It didn't take long for me to spot the guy going down the escalator. I ran down the stairs next to him.

"Hey! You won't believe it, but the cafe gave me my money back!" I exclaimed.

He looked at me, wide-eyed. "Oh, ok."

"You should go and get yours back too!"

He got off the escalator and I stood in front of him smiling, although I did briefly entertain the idea of sending his testicles into low-earth orbit. "I just thought I should find you and tell you! You don't want to lose two hundred yuan!"

"Yeah, I guess," he said, looking around. The woman walked over and said something to him in a hush, glancing at me.

I smiled at her too. "The weirdest thing happened. I

went back to the cafe and they were closed, but I knocked on the door and she gave me all my money back!"

"Huh," she said. "Maybe they were afraid of your beard."

"Come on! Let's go get your money back too!"

They looked at each other and agreed. And so we all walked off together pretending to be friends. I don't know what I expected to gain from this, but it did provide some small satisfaction.

They spoke to each other in rushed tones and started walking ahead of me. I walked along behind, smiling nonchalantly every time they looked back.

We arrived at the 'café' and finally the charade broke.

"Why are you following us?" the guy asked.

"What I want to know is when you get paid," I responded pettily, dropping the smile. "Is it now, or at the end of the day after you've sucked a few more people in?"

"Well done," the woman spat. "You're very smart. You have your money, so no problem. Go have a nice day."

I can never think of comebacks in the heat of the moment.

"Thank you. I will."

I walked back towards Tiananmen Square. The square is the heart of Beijing, China's answer to America's National Mall, and is a microcosmic demonstration of China's appetite for size. It is built around the Mausoleum of Mao Zedong, which is where Mao's waxy body lies in a glass box. The square is bordered to the west by the Great Hall of the People, an enormous palace that makes Buckingham look like a granny flat. On the east side of Tiananmen Square is the National Museum of China, an equally gargantuan palace that takes up almost fifteen acres of land. The square is bordered to the north by the first wall of the Forbidden City, instantly recognisable. An enormous portrait of Mao hangs over the gate.

Tiananmen Square is also infamous as the epicentre of student-led protests in 1989. The students were broadly protesting for democracy and freedom of speech but were mercilessly crushed by the Chinese military under the orders of the Communist Party leadership. Few people died in the Square itself but thousands were killed in the surrounding streets. They were shot, run over by tanks and beaten to death.

There are no monuments to the massacre, no plaque – in fact no memory at all. The Chinese government actively censors and suppresses any discussion of the event, meaning few young Chinese actually know that it happened. I stood there watching hundreds of people walking past me and taking photos of Tiananmen Square, queuing to see Mao's body, hailing a taxi, sitting in traffic, smoking, talking, laughing – how many of them knew what happened? I was tempted to shout it aloud but the thought was scared away.

The immense buildings flanking Tiananmen loomed higher under the shadow of a passing cloud as I turned and walked under Mao's portrait into the Forbidden City. I emerged into a huge tree-lined square, thronged by crowds.

The Forbidden City, to fill you in, was the home of China's emperors. It is a compound containing 980 palaces spread over 180 acres, all surrounded by a large wall and a wide moat to prevent peasants from entering. The last emperor to live there was Puyi, who abdicated in 1912.

Actually, while I was looking up these facts about the Forbidden City I got lost in a fascinating article about Puyi. The last emperor of China led an interesting life. After he surrendered the throne and left the Forbidden City, he moved to

Japanese territory in the city of Tianjin and became so bored that he grew addicted to shopping for pianos and watches. When the Japanese invaded China in 1931 he snuck into occupied Manchuria in the boot of a car, aided by his cousin, a bisexual cross-dresser named Eastern Jewel. The Japanese then allowed him to rule Manchuria as a puppet state. He stayed there until he was captured by the Soviets in 1945 and taken to Siberia with his servants.

In 1950, after negotiations between Mao and the Soviet Union, Puyi returned to China. He was imprisoned for ten years and 'remodelled' into a Communist. It was in prison, at the age of 44, that the once-pampered emperor first learned to brush his teeth and tie his shoes. After his release Puyi moved to Beijing with permission from Mao, where he worked under supervision as a street sweeper and a gardener. The last Emperor of China eventually returned to the Forbidden City in 1959 - but this time as a tourist, just one man in a large crowd staring at exhibits containing his own childhood toys.

Back to the story. I found an information panel with a map of the Forbidden City and took a moment to get my bearings, but couldn't find my location on the map. Confused, I looked around, back at the map, at the courtyard again and then back at the map. It wasn't on there. Maybe this map was wrong.

I walked through the rows of trees to the other side of the courtyard. There I saw a sign saying 'Tickets'. I whistled softly. The massive square I'd been admiring was only the ticketing area. I hadn't even entered the City itself.

I bought a ticket and walked towards the proper entrance underneath Beijing's perpetually smoggy sky. The red walls rose high above and occupied my entire field of vision. An Oriental palace of stacked, tapered roofs and gold lattice woodwork sat on the top of three archways leading into the city.

Strolling slowly, I emerged into another square that was easily the size of several football fields. The square was bisected by a river that curved in the shape of a bow. Five bridges spanned the river near the centre. I walked over one, running my hand along a weathered marble balustrade carved with images of dragons and other creatures. Beyond the river marble steps led up to a great hall guarding the entrance to whatever lay beyond.

I walked through and into a third square. This one totally dwarfed the first two. A strip of polished marble stones led down the centre, presumably once a walkway for the emperor, before rising into a set of stairs up a three-tiered carved marble base and into the largest palace I'd seen so far. This wooden monolith, standing thirty metres above the rest of the square, was China's throne room - the 'Hall of Supreme Harmony'.

I decided to head straight over the square, although it took at least five minutes to cross the immense expanse of stone. I climbed the stairs, sweating and occasionally pausing to look around at the crowds filling the square behind me. The tiled roofs of other palaces peeked out from between red walls and the lingering grey-blue smog above.

There was another large crowd of people at the top of the stairs jostling to see into the Hall itself. I entered the fray and was soon bustled to the front. I peered into the hall and found myself looking at the Dragon Throne, the seat of emperors. Carved of wood and inlaid with gold, it stood in the centre of the hall on a raised wooden podium between four gold pillars. The emperor would have had a long, uninterrupted view of anybody approaching across the square and up the stairs for many minutes before they eventually arrived and prostrated themselves at his feet.

One of the first things I noticed about China was the

country's sheer scale - the immense train stations, the number of people, the size of its cities. The Forbidden City really slammed this point home with each step over its man-made rivers, mighty gatehouses and vast marble squares towards a single chair sitting above it all, whose occupants once exercised unchecked control over the world's largest nation. That is, until the last became a street sweeper.

—

The morning brought what was now a familiar chill. Some shops near my hostel were selling steaming dumplings in bamboo containers. I ate some on the way to the first item on my agenda for the day - Mao's mausoleum (or as I prefer, the Mao-soleum).

I walked back to Tiananmen Square and got into the line to see Mao's corpse. The line passed through several security barriers and past some men selling bouquets of flowers. The mood of the queue soon became sombre. People stopped chatting to each other and put away their phones until the whole line became silent under the watchful eye of the guards posted around us. A few bought flowers and clutched them close while we walked up the stairs.

The line snaked into a quiet hallway, lined with banners and watched over by numerous guards, before moving into a small, dark room. Mao's body lay in a glass coffin in the centre. It was illuminated by the only light in the room and flanked by two motionless soldiers.

An older woman in front of me started sobbing uncontrollably at the sight of Mao's waxy body, lying as if he were asleep underneath a red flag emblazoned with a gold hammer and sickle. I glanced down at my flip flops and shorts, then around at the others in line wearing collared shirts, suits and jeans, then back to Mao's stiffened, preserved face.

We were quickly ushered through and out into the blinding daylight. The crying woman was consoled by her relatives. I hurried away.

The reverence that many Chinese once felt for Mao is hard to exaggerate. Take the story of the 'Mango Fever' that gripped China when Mao was gifted some mangoes by the Pakistani foreign minister in 1968. Mao sent the mangoes to universities and to factories, igniting a manic national obsession with the fruit. The mangoes, which few people in China had ever seen, soon became a symbol of Mao's 'generosity'. People gathered around the mangoes and "sang with wild abandonment." A poem was written in the fruits' honour that read, "again and again touching that golden mango, the golden mango was so warm." One mango was placed on an altar in a textile factory. When it began to rot it was boiled into a soup and fed to the factory workers. Another mango was sent on a specially chartered plane to a factory in Shanghai. Wax mango models toured through towns and cities, meeting enormous crowds everywhere they went. One unfortunate dentist in a small village made the mistake of comparing the holy fruit to a sweet potato. He was convicted of malicious slander and executed.

I spent the rest of the day in the National Museum, which is as big inside as it is outside, before returning to the same courtyard near my hostel for dinner. The white-aproned chefs smiled at me and shouted a greeting over the loud sizzle of the woks when I walked in. I smiled back and sat to eat and read my book. I had started reading the Lord of the Rings and soon became absorbed. The bustle around me faded into the background and a light rain pattered down on the corrugated plastic roof above, running away in lines that sparkled with a yellow light.

—

I set about preparing to travel to the Great Wall. When I say preparing, I bought a single packet of Oreos and a jar of honey from a supermarket, thinking I'd be able pick up bread or cereal from a town closer to the Wall, then went to sleep.

I woke to another chilly morning, ate some steaming dumplings and caught a bus towards a town called Huairou. There I was aiming to catch a rural bus, number 916, to get to a wild, semi-ruined stretch of the Wall.

Before the bus arrived in Huairou a man got on board. He saw me and motioned.

"Get off, here now."

I looked around at the other passengers, who were all Chinese.

"I'm going to Huairou," I said. We were parked outside of an industrial estate.

"Yes, this is it, you must get off."

I did as instructed. The bus doors closed with a clumsy clunk.

The man and five others immediately swarmed around. "Wall? Wall? Sixty dollar!"

"You've got to be kidding," I swore. I stormed off, swearing at both them and my infallible gullibility.

I had no idea where I was. The road dipped under a bridge ahead of me and industrial estates lay on both sides, all anonymous warehouses and expansive stretches of concrete reflecting a glaring sun.

For lack of a better idea I walked into one of these estates, past stacks of wooden pallets and waiting forklifts, to try and find someone who might help. I passed a red car parked between two warehouses and did a double-take. There was a guy sitting and smoking in the driver's seat.

I knocked on his window and he looked up with a

startled expression - as you would, I suppose, if you were a Chinese man enjoying a quiet smoke in a rural industrial estate somewhere north of Beijing and some sweaty white guy with a big red beard suddenly banged on your car window.

He rolled the window down cautiously.

"Bus 916?" I asked. He shook his head.

"Bus 916?" I mimed a steering wheel with my hands. He obviously didn't speak any English but it seemed futile to not make any noise at all.

He shook his head again.

I sighed and looked around. A stack of shipping containers sat at the far end of the yard in front of a spiked metal fence. The sun baked down, glaring bright off the concrete. I squinted, rubbed my eyes and looked back at the man. He was holding a pen and a yellow post-it note towards me.

I thanked him and promptly drew a terrible representation of a bus. He stared at it for a time and chuckled. I chuckled too. He turned to face me again and pointed back to the main road, indicating that I should turn right.

I thanked him and walked off, wiping my forehead. I passed under the bridge and came to a large roundabout that was planted with flowers. Then, miraculously, a bus with '916' in big letters on the front drove past me.

"Hallelujah," I muttered and plodded off in pursuit.

The 916 took me on a circuitous route through increasingly small villages and up steep hillsides covered in dense green forest. The other passengers disembarked one by one until I was left alone with a local couple and the bus driver.

The road narrowed and eventually ended in a small hamlet. The bus came to a juddering stop and we stepped out onto a dirt road, blinking in the bright sunshine. The Wall was visible, running along a high ridge to the south and continuing around the top of the valley before disappearing. The bus driver lit a cigarette while the couple walked up the road. There was nobody else there, except one old man who stared at me for a time before ambling slowly off. A donkey was tethered to a nearby house.

I needed to buy some water and food but the only store I could find was dark and locked. There was also a building that almost looked like a small hotel. I walked through the front door and into a white courtyard surrounded by doors. There was a large pallet of water bottles wrapped in plastic just nearby.

"Hello?" I called. There was no response. A small ginger cat skittered from one corner to another, where it sat and watched me warily.

"Hello?" I called again.

One of the doors opened and a bleary-eyed woman walked out. She rubbed her eyes and looked at me wordlessly.

"Ni hao," I said, smiling. I pointed at the water bottles. "Two?" I held up two fingers.

She nodded and took the money I offered.

"Food?" I asked.

She shook her head.

"Food anywhere?" I asked, pointing out the door.

She shook her head again, so I thanked her and stepped back outside. The driver sent up one last blue puff of smoke up towards a cloudless sky then started his engine and drove off. The donkey stood and watched me.

I gave up on finding any more food and set off on a dirt track heading towards the Wall, armed with two litres of water, ten Oreos and about 150 millilitres of honey in a small glass jar.

The path took me through a quiet forest for half an hour, through shaded wooden hallways and up steep riverbanks woven with knobbled tree roots, before it climbed suddenly upwards to a partially collapsed section of the Wall. I climbed to the top, turned left and started walking.

The Great Wall of China is another mind-blowing sight. It's one thing to read about it, like you are now, and another to see a line of rock five metres thick and ten metres high snaking along a steep, craggy mountain range from one horizon to the other. I could picture the Emperor standing down in the hamlet and saying, "I want a wall built on that mountain!" and all the peasants looking at each other thinking "oh for Pete's sake."

The Wall turned out to be more of a climb than a walk. This section was unrestored, left crumbling by the centuries and at many points overgrown with trees. It ran straight up and down the steep contours of the narrow, knife-like ridgeline, taking no shortcuts to avoid the steepest routes. I often found myself climbing vertically up rock faces, my pack pulling backwards at my shoulders and willing me to fall backwards.

The hills were steep teeth of rock, jagged shards that fell away occasionally to reveal sheer cliffs dropping down to the valley floor below. Watchtowers lay every few hundred metres on the peaks of the ridge – dark, forbidding forts with bricked up archways and black crevices.

In the mid-afternoon the Wall dipped into a saddle between two peaks and disappeared. I assumed it had been buried under the encroaching forest. A dirt path led into the trees for a short distance before it disappeared into dark square hole in the ground.

I dropped my pack into the hole, jumped after it and found myself in a dimly lit stone passageway. A large cat skittered out of an unseen corner and I jumped backwards with a curse, then lifted my pack again and trudged on.

As the sun started to drop I climbed up the steep flank of a hill and found a watchtower on the crest. The entrance to the watchtower was over two metres high, so a makeshift wooden ladder was propped up against the stone wall underneath. It was the only way up and was guarded by a middle-aged Chinese woman in a yellow jacket, exactly like a storybook troll guarding a bridge. She had a pudgy face, a nose that looked well-picked and a hanging gut. She watched me approach silently.

I went to use the ladder and she stuck out a hand.

"Five yuan."

I looked at her. "What?"

"Five yuan," she repeated, gesturing at the ladder. She then pointed at a small bag of beer cans. "Twenty yuan."

"I don't have five yuan." I dug out my remaining two yuan from my pocket. "This is all I've got."

She shook her head. "Five yuan."

Frustration took over. "Do you find it difficult to be a troll, or is it something that comes naturally?" I asked. She didn't speak English.

I showed her my empty pockets but Chinese Shrek refused to budge. I laughed aloud at how stupid this was. Here we both were, alone on a mountain and hours from anywhere with darkness setting in and she was going to charge me five yuan to use a wooden ladder.

There was no way I could go back and climb down some of those cliff faces in the dark. There was nothing for it but to push through. I moved to the ladder but she jabbered something and sat on the first rung, blocking the way.

I threw my pack up through the doorway, then grabbed the ledge to climb up the hard way. She made no move to stop me. After pulling myself up a little bit I decided this whole thing was a bloody joke and swung myself onto the ladder behind her. She stood and yelled, but it was too late.

I found a watchtower further on, the highest I could see

and decided to use it as a shelter for the night. I climbed to the top to see the view. Forested valleys ran away south with small villages running along their floors. One of these, I'd soon discover, was our little village of Pearl Springs. To the north lay nothing but sharp hills carpeted in green. The air was still smoggy, the horizon shrouded by a blue haze.

The tower I'd chosen was still largely intact, although a wall or two had fallen in. It had an ominous, dark feel and murmured with a voice of its own in the constant gusts of wind. I looked back over all the kilometres of Wall stretching away in both directions. Who was the Emperor so afraid of?

My stomach began rumbling. I drank the honey straight out of the jar and then spent a while with my mouth open around the rim and my head tilted back trying to get every last drop like a malnourished bear. I then spent some time reflecting on the quality of my decision-making, then moved onto the main meal - eight Oreos, rationed to one every ten minutes to make it seem like a real feast. I ate the last two Oreos fifteen minutes later for dessert.

I left the watchtower once darkness fell and nestled in against the battlements on the Wall to sleep. For all the mood and beauty of the place, however, it was not particularly practical. All the air moving up the side of the mountain rushed over the Wall in a constant roar of cold wind. It was like sleeping in an Arctic wind tunnel.

After a fitful few hours trying to sleep with my back pressed against the battlements, I moved back into the watchtower in complete darkness. The only sheltered spot inside was on the rubble of a collapsed wall. I contorted myself into position and closed my eyes, trying to ignore the stones pressing into my ribs and the moans and shrieks echoing in the solid darkness. And that is where you found me, shivering in the aching cold.

—

I woke early the next morning to more wind, drizzling rain and a temperature of about five degrees Celsius. I may as well have been naked for all the warmth my thin raincoat provided. I shivered uncontrollably, packed my bag with numb, stubby fingers and found myself, in a circular sort of way, longing to touch the warm torso of a Pakistani man.

I started off walking to warm myself up. The wall was treacherous in the rain. I took this opportunity to test the impact resistance of the stone a few times with my buttcheeks: I'm pleased to report that even after all these years, it's really very solid.

Eventually I arrived at a restored section of wall and an impassable watchtower. A path led down a crumbled section and onto a forest track that followed the Wall for a time before striking off downhill.

After another hour I finally found my way down the other side of the mountain and passed through several orchards to arrive in the quiet, peaceful village of Pearl Springs. I was getting understandably strange looks from the few villagers up and about.

"Huairou?" I asked a concerned-looking woman pushing a pram along the road.

She recoiled at the sight of me and hurriedly gestured towards a road through an orchard.

I thanked her and followed the small country lane through well-kept groves of walnut trees and small hamlets until I finally arrived at a major tourist area with chairlifts ferrying people up to the Wall. I bought a Snickers bar and some pot noodles from a food stall, which was all I could afford and sat at the ticket area clutching the steaming cup. People glanced twice at me as they walked past. There was honey in my beard, my pack was soaking wet, I was in nothing but shorts and a raincoat on a cold, wet day and my shoes were stained red with blood.

I walked back to a bus stop on the main road. A small, beat-up car soon pulled over. An elderly man sat in the driver's seat.

"Huairou?" I asked when he rolled down the window. He nodded and beckoned to get in. He drove me back to the bus stop. I returned to Beijing and feasted on hot, steamy dumplings until I could eat no more.

8
THE STEPPE

After spending a few days recovering in cafés and bookstores I collected my Mongolian visa and caught an overnight train to Hohhot, the capital of Inner Mongolia. It was a non-descript city of concrete blocks that did, bless it, have a KFC next to the train station. I then caught a bus packed full of boxes towards a small town on the Mongolian border named Erlian. The other passengers were a group of women who all knew each other. I put my headphones on and jotted a few notes in my journal.

Hohhot soon gave way to a flat, grassy plain. It was interspersed with tourist camps of white gers, the circular padded tents used by Mongolian nomads, although these soon petered out entirely. The only other signs of human activity were power lines rhythmically dipping and rising alongside the bus.

As the hours wore on and the women around me fell asleep one by one, the grass slowly became thinner until it eventually morphed into an endless expanse of sand, dotted with tiny green shrubs and divided by lines of fences marching straight towards an uncertain horizon. The wind whipped up columns of swirling dust.

The bus pulled into Erlian. A group of taxis were waiting to take us to the border crossing. I packed into one with a number of women from the bus and all of their boxes, squashed painfully against the window. The driver took us to the Chinese border post - a large, squat building underneath a huge arch painted in rainbow colours. He then inexplicably turned the car around and drove away from the border post, then pulled over five hundred metres up the road. We waited there for fifteen minutes. He then drove back to the border and let us go.

I left China, caught a waiting bus to the Mongolian building, cleared customs and stepped outside to wait for another bus that would take me to a nearby train station. The wind was blasting across the desert, whipping grains of sand that seemed to be stripping the skin from my arms. I found shelter with a group of others at a small bus stop. The blasting grit had almost completely stripped the paint from the metalwork. A chain link fence rattled violently as I looked around at this dusty outpost, weakly planted in an angry land.

The bus soon came and took us to the nearby town of Zamiin-Uud. A train sat idling on the tracks. I walked along the platform and into the ticket office. There was an old schedule on the wall inside, made of panels that updated every few minutes by flipping with a mechanical whirr. I stopped and stared at it, taken aback by the destination of the train waiting outside - Moscow.

I looked out a nearby window at the green carriages. I could be home in a fortnight. All I had to do was walk to the woman waiting behind the glass screen and say, "One ticket to Moscow, please." I stood for a minute, letting the wave of longing wash over me, then took a breath and walked up to the counter.

"One ticket to Ulaanbaatar."

The train was an overnighter. In a suspicious coincidence I was seated with an older English guy named Tony, the only other Westerner I'd seen since leaving Beijing. Tony had long grey hair and a wizened, solitary look. He was also nearly deaf. He ran a novelty shop back in the UK and had spent a few months in China buying trinkets to take back with him via the Trans-Siberian railway.

We spoke for a short while before settling in to our own

books. He had trouble hearing me over the train, but I wasn't chatty anyway. I was becoming more distant with people on the road, tired by the knowledge that the friendship would only last a few days before I'd be alone again. Staying alone was less effort.

The train clacked and clacked over a dusty yellow landscape. For a fleeting moment I was back on the Nullarbor watching dead tufts of grass slide past a dirty window, like a passing crowd stretching all the way back to the sandy horizon.

When I woke the next morning the sand had turned back into grass and the landscape was dotted with a steadily increasing number of circular white gers. The grass then turned into industrial yards and dirt roads before the train came to a slow, wheezy stop in Ulaanbaatar.

Tony approached while I was standing on the platform getting my bearings.

"Do you have a place to stay?"

"Not yet," I replied. "Do you know a good spot?"

"What?" He tilted his good ear towards me.

"DO YOU KNOW A GOOD SPOT?"

He nodded. "It's not far from here. Pretty central. Come with me if you like, although I have a reservation. They might be full."

I shrugged. "IT'S WORTH A GO."

We hoisted our packs and set off along the dual carriageway outside the station. The skyline was low and squat, mostly cubic apartment buildings. The cold air was gritty and the wind whipped up small whirls of dust as it blew past. The only colour in sight came from faded red 'Coca-Cola' signs above brick shopfronts. Most buildings had bars over their dark windows. I rubbed grit out of my eyes.

"Bit dismal, eh," Tony remarked.

"NOT THE BEST-LOOKING PLACE," I agreed.

"LOTS OF CONCRETE."

"It was all built in the space of about twenty years," Tony said, pointing at the rising buildings around us. "When the Soviets were here."

"IT DOES LOOK VERY SOVIET."

The guesthouse was up a small hill and along a dirt alleyway bordered by wobbly wooden fences and cracked cinderblock walls. It was run by a small, friendly older man, who had set up a number of gers on the roof. He had a spare bed for me – in fact, Tony and I were the only two guests he had.

He showed us to our ger. Six beds ringed a central stove and the heavy fabric ceiling was supported by spokes of wood radiating away from a hot chimney. The view from the rooftop looked out over a smoggy city of grey apartment blocks, concrete and small, leafless trees, all colours faded by grit and dust.

It was bleak, but there was a rush in my chest as I listened to the wind ripple and crack along the ger's fabric. I had dreamed of this country since seeing Ewan McGregor and Charley Boorman ride across the steppe in Long Way Round. Now I was here, standing in a cold breeze and looking out over a gritty, forgotten, unexplored city towards the promise of distant hills. I breathed in deep, bringing the cold into my lungs, and exhaled slowly.

—

It took two days to find my feet in Ulaanbaatar. I had no idea how to 'do Mongolia' and there seemed to be no good options. Other tourists I spoke with had done organised tours, which cost well upwards of $1800 for four or five days. Public transport was also a bad option. I would have to wait a day for a van to be packed full of people then sit in it for up to four days to arrive in a dreary provincial town with no further transport out into the steppe, where I really wanted to be. I was stuck.

I spent the first day walking for kilometres around Ulaanbaatar, wondering at the inexplicable absence of taxis. My destination was the famous Black Market, Naran Tuul, which isn't a black market in the conventional sense but an enormous open-air market. There were stalls selling clothes, shoes, saddles, bridles, materials to build a ger, tools, bow and arrows, antiques, swords, machetes, phones – everything.

I, however, was looking for a motorcycle. After running through the options it seemed the best way to get around Mongolia. It also meant I could experience the country as I'd first seen it through Ewan McGregor's helmet camera. I longed for the ability to set my own route, no longer beholden to buses and train lines. Yet the idea also tapped into something deeper. I think, at some level, it was also a challenge, some kind of primal urge to measure my own worth.

There were a number of motorcycle shops in Naran Tuul but these all sold Chinese brands known to fall apart for far more money than they're worth. Despairing, I left the market with sore feet and little to show for the day. The excitement of the night before had morphed into a simmering frustration. My time here was limited and I was so eager to get going that the thought of a wasted day was enough to bring down my mood.

There were a few taxis at the entrance, the first I'd seen in Ulaanbaatar, so I got one with four locals. The man sitting in the front passenger seat turned around.

"Where are you going?"

"Genghis Khan Square," I replied, relieved that someone could speak English.

He spoke to the driver in Mongolian then turned around again. He had a round face, short, cropped hair and was maybe thirty years old.

"How long have you been in Mongolia?"

"Just a day," I replied. "Got here off the train yesterday."

"Cool man, cool. What's your plan while you're here?"

"I'm not sure, trying to figure it out. I've got a month on my visa and was hoping of getting out into the countryside."

He thought for a moment. "Well, sometimes I help run tours into the country. I can give you some advice."

"Actually I'm on my way to the gym," he replied, "and if you come now I can introduce you to my friend and we can help you. He runs a tour company."

He shrugged. "No man, don't worry about it. I'm Bata, by the way." He extended his hand into the back of the cab.

"Ewen," I replied. He had a strong grip.

I soon found myself in a car park outside a sports complex that sat next to an empty canal of dry brown grass. I wrapped my jacket against the cold wind. Bata introduced me to his friend Amara.

I told them my budget and my rough plan, which was to go northwest to Khovsgul Lake, near the Russian border, where'd I'd heard it was possible to find nomadic reindeer herders. I'd then cross the country west to get to a town called Bayan Olgii, high in the Altai mountains, before continuing into Russia.

They looked at each other.

"Well, the bus to Olgii leaves once a week and takes four days," Bata said, turning to me again and scratching his chin. "Khovsgul is easier, but it is not possible to go from Khovsgul to the Altai by public transport. You have to fly or come back to Ulaanbaatar."

"That's what I've discovered," I said. "What are the

other options?"

"If you do not tour," said Amara, "you must..." He paused and spoke to Bata in Mongolian before continuing. "… you must buy something, a car, motorcycle, horse, or even bicycle."

Bata nodded in agreement. "Mongolia is very big and the transport is no good."

A gust of cold wind whirled dust around our feet. "I was thinking of buying a motorcycle," I said. "The only ones I could find were at Naran Tuul. All Chinese bikes."

Amara spoke to Bata again, who translated. "There is a place he knows where you can buy a motorcycle. Everyone in the countryside has one, the nomads. They have Chinese. But he knows a place that sells Japanese."

"Where?"

Bata looked it up on his phone. "Near this bridge," he said, "not far from the train station. It is closed now, maybe you go tomorrow."

I nodded in thanks and shook their hands. The sun was starting to drop, illuminating the few white clouds from beneath with an icy light.

"If you want," said Bata as he locked my hand in a vice, "I could meet you at Naran Tuul tomorrow, to help you buy equipment. My wife has a stall there."

"Great," I said. "Seems I got in the right cab!"

He laughed. "See you tomorrow man."

—

I walked straight to the motorcycle store the next morning along the same barren dual carriageway. The wind was still there and threw grit into my eyes as I walked the kilometres under another cloudless blue sky. The shop was exactly where

Bata had indicated, just across the road from a large Nissan dealership. A shrill bell rang when I walked in and caught the attention of a young guy in a black leather jacket.

"Hey man," he said in a soft voice. "You after a bike?"

"Yeah," I replied, extending a hand. The fact that he spoke flawless English was an unexpected relief. "I'm Ewen. Just having a look at what you've got."

"Gantur," he replied, shaking my hand. "Sure man, have a look. We've got these used bikes. What size are you after?"

"Nothing too huge," I said.

"Well these are the big ones," Gantur said. The tiled shop floor displayed a range of used motorcycles, from an old blue Suzuki sports bike up to a massive BMW GS Adventure - the same bike Ewan McGregor rode.

He walked me down to the BMW. "This is 1200cc, which is too big I'm guessing. What's your budget?"

I laughed. "The budget is low. Very low."

"What are you using the bike for?"

I explained my plan. Gantur looked at me for a moment and laughed.

"Dude, you're crazy. You can't ride a bike from here to Olgii. It's not possible."

I shrugged. "Maybe not, but I don't know that yet. What else have you got?"

Gantur walked me back down the line to another BMW that was also far too expensive. I kept walking, eyeing and dismissing each price tag in turn.

Right down the cheap end, however, there was a thin white Honda. It was an old, unassuming, dusty motorcycle plastered in Dunlop stickers with chipped bodywork, a small, mud-spattered engine and cracked, worn tires. The square headlight sat high over the front wheel, like a child straightening himself against a measuring stick.

"How much is this one?" I asked, placing a hand on the seat.

"That one?" Gantur asked. "Four million tugrik." Roughly $2000.

I swung my leg over onto the seat and felt the bike sink as the suspension took my weight. "How is it?"

"It's alright," said Gantur. "Not our best. Used, needs new tires, but it is a good bike, good engine and that's what matters. Honda are reliable, you won't find a better bike in Ulaanbaatar for that price."

I did a few basic checks. I didn't know a whole lot about bikes but had previously owned one and knew the basics of what to look for. Or at least I thought I did. I rolled the bike forward and squeezed the front brake, then rolled it back and pressed the back brake with my right foot. It wasn't the best but it was the only one they had that fit my budget. My choice became apparent. I could buy this worn Honda or a slightly cheaper Chinese bike from a dodgier dealer in Naran Tuul.

"If I'm going to buy one, it'll probably be this one," I said. "I'll give you three and a half for it. It's got a few issues, starting with the fact that it needs new tires. I also need somewhere to strap a pack."

Gantur thought for a moment and put a hand on his chin. A shadow passed outside as a cloud drifted in front of the sun.

"I'll have to check with the boss, but 3.5 is probably too low. We don't make much on these used bikes. Although we do need to get rid of this one."

"I can take it off you as soon as its ready. Just see what you can do, I'd appreciate it."

Gantur left to speak to the boss, a sharp-eyed guy in an orange jumper who had been watching from across the shop floor. After a quick chat they both walked back over.

"He says he can do 3.7 million, but he'll also change the tires, service it, get you the right paperwork from the government and put a rack on the back so you can strap your pack on."

That was exactly what I needed to hear.

"Awesome! Thanks man. I need an evening to think it over, but I'll let you know tomorrow if you put it aside." I shook the boss's hand with a smile as Gantur translated.

I had given myself time to process the decision, but deep down I knew that it had already been made. I was going to try and cross Mongolia on this small white Honda: and so, I began my turbulent relationship with a little rattling motorcycle that was older than I was, had an engine roughly the size of a small lawnmower and liked to fall to bits.

The boss left to speak to another customer. Gantur hung around.

"How come you're in Mongolia, anyway? Why are you doing this crazy trip?"

"I'm actually trying to get from Australia to Switzerland without flying," I said. "So I guess I'm about halfway there."

Gantur took his cap off and ran a hand through his hair. "Dude. I'd love to do something like that."

"Why don't you?" I asked. "Could you save the money?"

"I could, but like, I'm just working this shitty job. I can't wait to find something else and get out of here."

"What are you looking for?"

He looked around and sighed as he adjusted his cap.

"I actually studied in the US. I was hoping to find work after my degree, but ran into legal issues with my visa so I had to come back to UB. Been working here since, but man, I don't know. There's not much work here, you know?"

"It's a small city." I was unsure what to say. "Is there any chance you could study overseas again? Maybe back in the US?"

Gantur looked out the window and shook his head. "Maybe, man. I'd love to study there again. But I don't know. It's not easy to make that decision, you know? You're lucky you're not from here."

"It's an option though?"

"Could be, could be. I'd just love to do something like what you're doing."

I thought for a moment. I wasn't really sure what I was doing. I needed a motorcycle, so here I was.

"I'm lucky that I was able to save the money for it," I said slowly. "But the hardest part, I think, was deciding to do it. Continuing has been fairly straightforward."

"You're probably right," Gantur said. "I've gotta get out of this shop."

"Thanks again for your help mate. I'll see you tomorrow."

—

It took another four days to get the bike ready to go. I met Bata each day, either at Naran Tuul or in the city for a drink. He went far out of his way to help me. Together we navigated the market and he negotiated prices down on a jacket, boots, clothes, tools - everything I needed to ride west. He also advised me to buy cigarettes, lighters and lollipops as gifts for the herders. In return, on one evening I helped him pick up his drunk father-in-law from a karaoke bar somewhere in Ulaanbaatar's tent suburbs; an intricate maze of dirt alleyways, wooden fences, barking dogs and circular white gers, smoke rising from every chimney. Bata also fed me at his apartment, a small place across the railway line with a view over rusty industrial estates.

I also met Gantur to check on the bike. He brought me with him to a mechanic deep in the smoky ger streets where we helped two young boys service the bike and fit a rack just wide enough to take my pack and two spare tires. Gantur also introduced me via text to a young French guy named Jean, who was heading to Kazakhstan on a hefty BMW.

I arranged to meet Jean for a coffee to discuss the road ahead. He had been preparing his bike for weeks, which made me wonder privately if I had severely underestimated the task I'd just set myself.

One day, while I was waiting for word from Gantur, Jean kindly offered to take me on the back of his bike to the famous statue of Genghis Khan. It was located some way out of Ulaanbaatar – a towering silver monolith of Mongolia's most famous son, mounted and staring quietly over the sprawling plains with his right arm raised as if to order the hordes forward. The noise of Jean's engine was drowned out by the roaring wind. Sitting on the back of Jean's bike, gripping the seat, I had my first close exposure to the steppe - that empty, formidable expanse of thunderous clouds and thin grass, angry and powerful, almost like a bear lifting itself on its hind legs in challenge when we rushed past.

On the fourth day I went to the shop. The last step was to register the bike with the government and get a license plate. The shop ran on Mongolian time, so I thumbed through motocross magazines for two hours before the boss finally got around to helping us. We didn't finish until ten that evening.

I won't go into too much detail, but that day takes the cake for the most bureaucratic experience of my life. Here's an example to give you an idea of the sort of hoops we had to jump through. When the bike entered Mongolia, at some point in the indeterminate past, a mechanic had written an inspection report claiming that the bike was red. This was despite the fact that it was clearly, indisputably, white. It had never been red. There wasn't a red patch on it. The lady sitting behind the solid wooden desk in a dark, dank office somewhere in the government's lair, however, insisted that the bike must be red.

"How can the bike be white when the paperwork says that it is red?"

"It's not red, trust me," Gantur said. "It's white." He showed her a photo on his phone.

"Well, we can't change the paperwork," she replied in halting English, looking over her glasses. "The bike must be red."

Gantur groaned and turned to face me. "I don't know what to do about this."

I rubbed my temples slowly, thinking. "Well, we can't change the paperwork. So I guess we have to change the bike. Know anywhere we can buy spray paint?"

Gantur sighed. "That could work. I'm sorry man. This is typical Mongolia."

The lady wasn't done. She refused to issue me a license plate, claiming that the paper transit license I'd been given was enough.

Gantur leaned over. "Don't worry, I'll sort that out," he said quietly. "Just wait outside for a few minutes."

I stood outside the building in the ever-present cold

wind and suppressed a rising sense of frustration and urgency. All I want is to be out on the steppe, I thought. Is it really that hard? Maybe I'll spend a week or more in Ulaanbaatar, waking up in my rooftop ger in freezing temperatures to a cacophony of barking dogs and running through an icy, biting wind to the outhouse and into a cold, dribbling shower.

Gantur soon reappeared with a victorious smile. He was followed by a short thickset man with a wrinkled face.

"He'll make one for you, but you have to pay him."

The man looked around warily.

"Thank god," I said, releasing a deep breath. "Sure. If that's what it takes." I fished a wad of cash out of my jacket pocket and pressed it into the man's hand.

He quickly tucked it away and disappeared back into the drab building.

"How'd you do it?" I asked Gantur once the man had gone.

Gantur chuckled. "I told him my strange foreign friend wanted a souvenir."

I laughed in relief. "You live in a funny country, you know that?"

"Ugh," he groaned, rubbing his eyes. "Sometimes it frustrates me so much."

We returned to the shop to paint the bike. Just when the sun was throwing a dimming orange light into Ulaanbaatar's smoggy sky, it was ready. The shitty white Honda was now a shitty red Honda.

Gantur and I grinned at each other and hugged. "I can't thank you enough," I said, putting a hand on his shoulder. "If I get home in one piece it's only because of your help."

He chuckled. "I still don't think you'll get there. You're crazy, man, riding across Mongolia on this. I think it will break down. But good luck."

The boss came over to see me off. He spoke to Gantur for a moment, then stuck out his hand. I shook it and Gantur translated.

"He says you're fucking crazy, but he likes you. A real man. He says good luck, keep the tires on the ground, make sure to change the oil every two thousand kilometres."

I grinned. "I'll try."

We fetched my pack and strapped it on. It sat haphazardly on a rack that was only just wide enough, but Gantur's boss tied a rope around to keep everything secure. The loaded pack meant I couldn't swing my leg over the bike, so I lifted my foot over the seat and awkwardly hopped into position.

"Gonna name it?" said Gantur. I pressed the switch. The engine came to life with a few wheezy puffs and sent a weak pulse through the handlebars. I looked down at the scratched speedometer. The needle vibrated gently.

"Noddy," I said. "I think I'll call it Noddy."

9
THE ROAD

I didn't get much sleep that night. The anticipation put me on edge. Each flap of the fabric was a reminder of the wind fighting to get in. Sleep, when it came, was ended early by my alarm.

I walked to the outhouse for the last time in a grey dawn light, my breath foggy in the cold air, and endured my last dribbly, icy shower while quickly losing sensation in my toes. After spending twenty minutes trying to load my pack and spare tires onto Noddy I brought him coughing to life. I put my helmet on, feeling the new weight on my neck, and wobbled off down the dirt alleyway. The neighbourhood dogs roused quickly with the usual cacophony of throaty barks.

Things started going wrong from the first minute. Neither the speedometer nor the odometer actually worked. I had somehow failed to notice either of these things on a test drive several days earlier. This meant that Noddy had possibly done 90,000 km, or 190,000. I also had no idea how fast I was going - which in truth wasn't fast at all.

I brushed aside the annoyance and instead dwelt on the fact that I was finally leaving Ulaanbaatar. It was a gritty, bleak city, but in a way I had come to like it. I had begun to build a small network of friends – Bata, Gantur, Jean – and through them had enjoyed a home-cooked meal and spent my time hanging around in cafés, bars, mechanics' workshops, market stalls. It wasn't impossible to see myself settling in, coming to see the Soviet-style city with its grit and cold winds as some kind of home.

I kept my eyes on the road. The morning air leaked

through my zippers and tickled my bare skin with cold fingers. I planned to head west along a paved main road, then turn off north and follow another main highway towards Khovsgul Lake, almost a thousand kilometres by road. I'd based this plan on Google Maps, which confidently displayed the highways as nice thick lines. The steppe opened before me and beckoned with wide open arms when Noddy and I left the outskirts of Ulaanbaatar.

It's difficult to describe the Mongolian landscape. It's one thing to look at pictures of it, another thing to see it from a distance and something else entirely to be immersed and alone in the sheer emptiness.

Imagine, for a moment, that you're a small mouse, adrift on a bit of wood in the middle of a stormy ocean. Look around at the waves taller than buildings, crested in white as they roll past and lift you far up into the mighty wind and down again. Now freeze the image. Make the waves a windswept green colour, crest them with rocky outcrops and add dappled sunlight amidst passing curtains of grey rain, so that some of the landscape is in shadow and some is in light. That is Mongolia.

I rode through this oceanic landscape for a while. The emptiness was interrupted only by nomadic herders on horseback watching over their herds of horses and yaks and by circular white ger tents dotting the plains like little white cheesecakes.

After a few hours I reached my turn off, which is where things went wrong again. It was just a rocky dirt track wobbling up into the hills. I checked my location on a map I'd downloaded onto my phone. This was definitely it – this must be what highways look like in Mongolia. I turned off the road. It was the first time I'd ever ridden a motorcycle on anything other than asphalt.

I followed the tracks up into the hills. Noddy shuddered violently on the rough ground and I weaved my way past the largest rocks, seeking the path that seemed least likely to shake him to pieces. He didn't have a fuel gauge and the broken odometer meant I couldn't count the kilometres we'd travelled. All I knew was that he had a 200-kilometre range with an extra thirty kilometres in the reserve tank. I also had a small jerry can underneath my pack that could give another hundred kilometres in a bind.

Eventually I stopped at the crest of a hill to decide whether to press on. The land dropped away before me into a shallow green valley that was cut along its length by a dry riverbed. A line of serrated brown hills lay on the horizon, fading into blue beyond. A dust plume rose on the distant road. It was heading towards me.

I waited as it tracked along and eventually became a Jeep, then flagged it over.

"Benzene?" I asked when the occupants wound down the window, pointing in the direction they'd come.

The woman in the passenger seat shook her head. She then looked at Noddy, smiled and pointed at him, holding up two fingers on the other hand and speaking in excited Mongolian.

"Tugrik?"

She nodded vigorously. The man in the driver's seat leaned over with a smile.

"Honda!" he exclaimed, holding up two fingers and shaking them for emphasis. "Tugrik!"

I laughed and shook my head. "Sorry!"

They shrugged and drove off slowly to avoid covering me in a cloud of dust.

I looked at the road ahead. It seemed to become progressively rockier as it thinned towards the distant hills.

There was no telling how far it went before another town. I was having difficulty adjusting to riding a motorcycle off-road, let alone over large rocks. I decided that continuing wasn't worth the risk of breaking Noddy or myself, or running out of fuel.

I turned Noddy around and rode back towards Ulaanbaatar, muttering inside my helmet. On the way back I hit a bump in the road and the cover of Noddy's rev counter flew off. I pulled over and stormed up and down the side of the highway for twenty minutes before giving up, fuming while I rode for three hours back along the same road.

At nearly ten in the evening, just when darkness finally fell, I pulled over to set up camp at the base of a gently sloping hill. I'd been riding all day and was only a hundred kilometres from where I'd started.

I put Noddy's kickstand down and lowered his weight gently, when suddenly he fell onto his side. I swore aloud, ripped my pack off the back and heaved him upright to check the damage. He'd snapped his clutch handle. We were immobile.

I swore again, putting my hands on my head and looking around in the vain hope that the solution was lying on the ground nearby. A knot rose in my throat. The guys in Ulaanbaatar were right. This was crazy. I can't fix a motorcycle or ride off-road. I don't even have the right tools. Why did I think I could ride across Mongolia? I'm alone and inadequate in the face of this task. How will this end?

Despairing, I decided there was nothing to do until daylight. I pitched my little black tent, just big enough to lie in, used my jacket and wool-lined sweater as a pillow and listened to podcasts while the knot in my throat slowly loosened.

I was woken in the middle of the night by distant howls. My eyes opened wide and my hand strayed to my small pocketknife, but the steppe went quiet.

My heart thumped to life a short while later at the eerie sound of sniffing near my head. I lay perfectly still, taking shallow, quiet breaths. The sniffing eventually stopped. I drifted back to sleep.

—

I woke to daylight, blinking slowly. The bit of hope that I'd wake up at home quickly drowned when I remembered where I was. This wasn't just a bad dream. I was still in Mongolia, lying on the ground, alone and immobile on a freezing morning, thousands of kilometres yet to go and Noddy's clutch handle was still broken.

I rubbed my eyes and unzipped the tent. Three small horses stood motionless a few metres away and stared at me intently. The sun cast a gentle sideways light, catching their coats in the same faded yellow as the grass underneath. One snorted and sent steam into the morning air.

I stood up and looked around. A wall of white was blowing across the grasslands from the north. A snowstorm. Wonderful.

I pulled some duct tape out of my pack and tried strapping the clutch handle together. It didn't work. I swore softly and the despair of the night before welled in my chest.

Then, from over the crest of the hill, a man in robes trotted up on a horse and sent the other three scattering, whinnying nervously.

"Sanbainuu," I said in pidgin Mongolian. He stared at me silently. I pointed at the clutch handle. He stared at that silently too. After a few more minutes of gazing silently at each other and at Noddy, he turned his horse and trotted off, back over the hill.

I finished packing then boiled water to have a coffee and warm my hands while pondering my next move. Just when I was about to start pushing Noddy back towards the distant road another guy zoomed over the hilltop on a motorcycle. He looked at the clutch handle and pointed to the back of his bike. Flurries of snow were blowing in on a strengthening wind, erasing our surroundings in a white blur.

I hopped on. He took off and we flew across the steppe. Snow blew in my face and stuck to my beard while I clung on for dear life. A herd of horses suddenly appeared out of the white. The man circled them a few times. I clung on, trying to keep my arse on the seat as he leaned this way and that, flying into ditches and launching out again.

We then shot off in another direction and soon arrived at an empty ger camp. Two enormous, wolf-like dogs loped over and chased the motorcycle as we pulled in, barking ferociously and showing pointed canines the length of my little finger. The owner of the camp came out and yelled in a booming voice. He was a heavy man and was wearing a brown camouflage jacket and military-style boots. The dogs quietened. The two men spoke together in Mongolia, before the owner turned to me while I dismounted.

"Your bike is broken?"

"Yeah, about a kilometre that way." I indicated where I thought it was, somewhere in the flurrying white.

He motioned for me to get back on the man's motorcycle. I was whisked back to Noddy with some tools. The snow was blowing thicker and it was difficult to hear each other over the rushing wind. The man made an impromptu clutch handle out of the remnants of the old one and a spare they had in the camp, then tried to get Noddy to start. He refused.

The man rode off back to camp and returned with the owner in a flatbed truck. Together we hoisted Noddy on and hauled him back to a shed. He needed new spark plugs. I had some spares in my pack.

"Where are you heading?" the owner asked in the gruff voice once Noddy was functioning.

"Up to Khovsgul," I replied. "Is this the right road?"

He nodded. "You will have to wait though. It is not possible to ride in this weather. Bad snowstorm. From Siberia."

I agreed. The snow was swirling around the camp and had begun to cover the ground in a white frosting.

"And after Khovsgul?"

"Bayan Olgii," I said. "I will stay near Khovsgul a few days and then take the northern road from there. Do you know it?"

"To Olgii?" He scratched his head. "I don't think that is possible. That bike cannot go to Olgii. You need a car."

I looked at Noddy leaning nonchalantly on his kickstand. "I'd love a car, but don't have the money. The bike will have to do. Do you know if the northern road is good?"

He thought for a moment. "I have not done that one, but I know another road. Further south. The northern road may not be possible. When you get to Khovsgul, you can ask. They will tell you the way."

"I will," I said. "I'm finding that maps here aren't so reliable."

"No, Mongolian maps aren't good. The roads change every year. You must ask."

We were silent for a moment as a gust of wind rattled the roof. The shed creaked under the strain.

"This is your camp?"

He nodded. "Now, no people, but in summer I am very busy with tourists. Lots of Chinese. If you want, you can stay in a ger until the snow is finished."

And so, within two hours of waking up in the freezing

cold in the middle of nowhere with an immobile motorcycle, I was in a warm ger with a hot pot of tea and biscuits, a fire going in the central stove and a newly functioning Noddy. I took my boots off, lay my wet socks near the fire to dry and stretched out on a bed to read my book. The snowstorm blew past, murmuring angrily and rattling the door.

I rode the rest of that day along decent roads. Every so often I stood on the pedals to relieve my aching buttocks. The landscape rolled by and became greener as I travelled north.

Eventually the icy wind forced me to pull into a roadside café to warm up. A small man greeted me excitedly when I entered through a pair of swinging wooden saloon doors.

"Deutsch?" he asked. I sat down. We were alone in the room.

I looked at him, shocked. "What? You speak German? Sprechen Sie Deutsch?"

"Ja!" he exclaimed. "Ich spreche Deutsch!"

I couldn't believe it. Here I was, in a small, dark, dusky roadside café somewhere in rural Mongolia, approaching the border with Siberia and this guy speaks German.

We spoke for a while and although my German wasn't great I learnt his story. He had worked in a restaurant in Dresden for a few years before returning to Mongolia because of visa issues. He had also missed the vast open spaces and found Germany a bit too crowded.

I took the opportunity to ask him about the northern road. He looked at my map, which I'd bought in Naran Tuul with Bata. It looked like the sort of colour-coded map you'd find in a primary school classroom. I'd chosen it over a proper one because it was labelled in Mongolian, so I could use it to get directions from locals who knew the current roads and conditions.

Unfortunately the German-speaking man couldn't tell me much. I thanked him, warmed up with a hot tea and then set out again to do battle with the wind.

A few hours later, while the sun was setting, I arrived at an intersection with a gas station on one corner and a small abandoned building on the other. The road I was on continued to Russia. I turned left and leaned Noddy into the curve. The reflection of his orange indicator light blinked off a nearby sign in the growing darkness. It was at this unremarkable place that, for the first time since crossing Australia, I finally turned west. I pointed Noddy's weak headlight towards Switzerland and putted along underneath dark clouds that speared across the sky, searching for a place to set up camp.

—

The following morning I arrived in Erdenet, Mongolia's second city, and stopped at a supermarket for some food. Then, just when I was set to leave, Noddy refused to start. I pressed the on switch a few times and only heard a muffled click.

I took a deep breath and got off to troubleshoot. Within a minute two men came over to have a look. One had a toolkit on him and quickly worked out that the problem was a faulty fuse. The other guy hill-started the bike.

I rode Noddy through Erdenet looking for a mechanic and found one on the far side of town. One of the men working there knew a few words in English.

"The fuse is broken," I said, pointing to the battery. "Can you fix it?"

He stooped down for a quick look, then nodded and pointed over the road.

"Ok," I indicated the makeshift clutch handle.

"Yes, is possible. Must... uh..." He looked around for inspiration, then pointed over the road and mimed a steering wheel. "Zakh."

"Market?" I asked and pointed at the speedometer. "New?"

He nodded. "No problem, no problem."

I spent the afternoon at the mechanics and helped him dismember Noddy and piece him together again. We drove in his rattling car to a local market to look for parts. The town wasn't much, just a number of dirty apartment blocks stretched along the length of a single main road with outskirts of white gers squatting in fenced compounds amongst a makeshift network of potted dirt tracks. A large open-cut mine was just visible on a nearby hillside. There were no trees.

After buying some wires at the market the mechanic took me to a welder's shack to piece the clutch handle back together. The floor was littered with the dirty, dead bowels of old machinery, the walls black with soot and grime. Smoke hung in the air. The welder lowered an iron mask and set to work, stopping occasionally to dunk the handle in a bucket of brown water with a searing hiss. It reminded me a little of Star Wars, of a grungy workshop on some erratic desert planet, workers welding hobbled spaceships back together with white flashes of light and arcing streams of red sparks.

We didn't finish fixing Noddy until late that evening.

"You go?" the mechanic asked.

I looked at the night sky. "Yes, but not far."

He pointed at a couch in the workshop. "Here? No problem." He made a pillow with his hands.

"Are you sure?"

"Yes, I sorry, here is only place." He rocked his arms as if he was holding a baby, ran a finger down his cheeks to mimic tears, then pointed at himself.

"You have a baby at home?"

"Yes, baby. I no sleep, every night, no sleep. Not possible for you, sleep," he said. "I very sorry."

"It's ok, it's ok," I said with a smile. "No need at all, the couch is perfect. Much better than the ground." I pointed at the couch and gave a thumbs-up.

He looked at me doubtfully. "You are sure?"

"Yes, yes, no problem. Thank you so much for today. Good luck with your baby!"

He smiled and extended a hand. "Thank you! You go good to Olgii!"

After he left I locked up, settled in on the sunken couch and soon fell asleep to the sound of the whistling wind.

—

A huge bang on the door woke me with a start. I sat bolt upright and scrambled for my phone to get some light. The door crashed again.

"Just a sec!" I yelled, scrambling to put on some pants with a surge of adrenalin. What time is it? Is it the morning? There was no light coming through the windows. I opened the door, shirtless. Two men were standing in the darkness. I felt another surge of adrenalin and the muscles in my legs and chest tightened reflexively.

"Sanbainuu," one of the men said. The other wobbled unsteadily.

"Sanbainuu," I said warily. I kept one hand on the door, ready to slam it shut. My heart pulsed against my ribs. "What do you want?"

"You have... motorbike?" the man asked, mimicking a throttle. The other guy leaned forward precariously. "I am cousin of mechanic... cousin!"

"Why are you here?" I asked. "It's the middle of the night."

"My friend, he very drunk." The other guy giggled. "I use bike, he go home. Five minute! Five minute!"

"You want to use my bike to take him home?" I repeated, relaxing a fist that I hadn't realised I'd made.

"Yes! Yes! Five minute!" He became more excited. I stood still in the doorway and shook my head.

"I can't let you use my bike," I said. "That's not possible."

"WHY? Only five minute! Not far!" The drunker guy groaned, swaying. "I am cousin! Let you sleep here!"

I stepped back from the door. The man doing the negotiating flicked a nearby switch to turn the lights on and became even more excited upon seeing Noddy resting on his kickstand.

"Five minute! Why not? Why you not let me go?" He raised his voice and walked towards me.

I stood my ground in a surge of frustration. "I'm sorry, the risk is too much. Maybe I can take him?"

He shook his head. "No, I take, I take! Five minute! We let you fucking sleep here! Why not you help me?"

I thought for a moment. I was unsure how to make them leave. The thought of lending them Noddy even flickered through my mind as I tried to think of a solution, but was replaced by anger. What right did they have to my motorcycle? Why am I awake at this stupid hour?

"No," I said again. "My answer is no. I'm sorry. It is my bike and the risk is too much."

"No! FUCKING WHY!" he yelled. The drunker man groaned loudly and swayed while he stood near the door.

"FIVE MINUTE! ONLY FIVE FUCKING MINUTE! NO PROBLEM! WHAT IS PROBLEM?" He punched the corrugated wall of the workshop and sent a slamming metallic echo through the shed. The anger surged again. I snapped.

"My answer is NO!" I raised my voice to match his and took a few steps towards him. "I'm not just going to lend my motorcycle to some random! I don't even know who you are! You claim to work here but I have no idea if you're just here to steal my bike. Both of you need to GET OUT!"

He was taken aback by the outburst and took a few paces back. "I am cousin!" he appealed in a calmer voice. "Must go home!"

I shook my head and pointed at the door. "I can give you money for a taxi. It's time to go."

I walked over to the drunker guy and guided him towards the door. He obliged with a moan. The friend followed shortly after and I stood in the doorway again, pleased that they were out of the workshop. I pulled a small bit of cash out of my pocket.

"Here, for taxi."

"No taxi!" he said. There was an edge on his voice. "No taxi here!"

"Then you'll just have to fucking walk, won't you."

He accepted the money and grabbed his friend. The pair wobbled off into the darkness.

"Jesus." I let out a lungful of air, suddenly aware of the cold.

My phone lit up when I lay back in my sleeping bag.
"Goodnight."
Goodnight Vilai.

—

I set off again as the sun was rising. Noddy was running smoothly and road was easy. The grasslands rose steadily into rolling green hills that in turn grew into fertile green valleys flanked by tree-covered slopes, occupied only by log cabins sitting beside wide rivers. Every so often I could see herds of goats tended by shepherds on horseback. They eyed me from a distance.

Everything was going well, although I was getting slightly bored. I was, after all, alone with my thoughts inside a motorcycle helmet with just the noise of the wind for company. Sometimes it played a sort of tenor tune when it rushed through my helmet, a mid-range whistle, before cutting in with a soprano overlay like a whistling kettle. I started whistling in harmony for a while. I also sang to myself. It's actually difficult to remember song lyrics without being prompted by music. I ended up swapping between the first few verses of Dani California and some national anthems.

In the afternoon I pulled over to make a tea next to a small river. A log cabin sat in woods on the other side, surrounded by spring flowers. As I sat, waiting for the water to boil, a man on a heavy Chinese motorcycle pulled over. His wife was seated on the back holding their baby daughter wrapped in blankets. They were both wearing traditional Mongolian deel, which look like a bit like thick padded dressing gowns. His was pink and hers was a deep royal blue.

He dismounted, looked at my bike, then looked at me.

"Sanbainuu," I said. He patted the bike and held a thumb up. I copied. He nodded.

I pointed at the boiling water and mimed a drink. He nodded again and sat cross-legged. His wife came and sat next to him.

I stood up to fetch the tea from my pack and knocked the pot over, sending steaming water all over the ground. They looked at me. I laughed and put another pot on, then went to get the tea.

The man tapped my shoulder as I was rifling through

my pack. I turned around. The rubber handle of the pot had caught fire and my whole set up was in flames. I blew it out and then took a brief moment to think about to the fact that they, quite accurately, had likely diagnosed me as a total moron.

Which is, incidentally, the name of the town we were heading towards. Murun in some spellings, Moron in others. Honestly. I knew I was going to feel right at home there so I was keen to get going, but the man motioned for me to go with them in convoy. He pointed at me and made a pillow with his hands.

I accepted and followed them at fifty kilometres per hour, his bike's top speed. I bought them lunch at an isolated roadside shop and tried making some conversation, but the language barrier was difficult and they weren't particularly interested in talking.

In the late afternoon, as we crossed a hilltop in a ferocious wind, the man suddenly pulled over. His tyre was flat. I helped him change it over, but while we were doing that Noddy toppled over in a gust of wind. I swore aloud. The clutch handle had broken along the welded seam. Luckily I could just manage to change gears using what was left. We packed up and pressed on.

—

The hours passed and the steppe changed its mood. Far in the distance, great rain giants strode southwards and dragged their grey legs over angry, jagged hills. The wind strengthened again, roaring past in fury and causing Noddy to wobble unsteadily as we motored along.

As the sun approached the horizon we crested a hill and finally saw Moron sprawled along a wide, marshy plain and ringed by rippling hills. A small river ran through the marshes, reminding me of winding blue ribbons lying on a soft green carpet.

The man led me to a small house surrounded by a tall wooden fence. He indicated that I should wait, so I sat on Noddy while he and his wife disappeared inside. A dog started barking. Some local kids playing with a soccer ball further down the alley stopped and pointed at me. A young girl dusted in dirt sucked her thumb and stared.

The man returned shortly and held up eight fingers.

"Tugrik," he said, then made a pillow with his hands.

"How much?" I asked, pulling out a 10,000 tugrik note. He pointed at it, then held up eight fingers again.

"Eighty thousand tugrik? To stay?" I shook my head. "No thanks."

He shrugged and shook my hand. "Thank you, thank you."

I motored off and set up camp on the far side of town. The wind was blowing steadily from the north so I sheltered my tent next to a fence on the marsh's edge. I made some hot noodles and watched local herders ride back out of town. The weak headlights of their motorcycles turned from side to side in the growing darkness as they searched for pathways through the reeds.

—

I was woken during the night by heavy footfalls near my tent. Mongolia suffers from rampant alcoholism and alcohol-related violence and drunk men are often visible on the streets. I thought I'd chosen a well-hidden spot but was clearly wrong.

I lay still, hoping the guy was sober or at least uninterested in my tent. My hand unconsciously strayed to my pocketknife in search some sort of reassurance.

Suddenly a hand pushed on the tent fabric and grabbed my foot. I shot upright and my heart slammed into action as I ripped the sleeping bag off, expecting a knife to rip through the tent at any moment. I pushed the tent flap outwards and saw the man wobbling off and chuckling to himself. I breathed a sigh of relief, dropped the little pocketknife and flopped back onto my folded woollen jumper. It took some time to fall back asleep on the hard ground.

10
THE FOREST

I found the local tourism centre the next morning, hoping to get some information about how to find the reindeer herders. It was dark and the door was locked. I stood there a moment, pondering the next decision and heard someone speak in a loud American voice nearby.

"How much more is there?" she asked. "I think it's almost done."

I turned around and saw a short, solid woman directing a Mongolian man while he stacked boxes into the back of a small car.

"Oh, hi there!" she said, noticing me. "Can I help you with something? Do you speak English?"

"Hi, and yes," I said. "I was hoping to get some information about the reindeer herders but the office is closed."

"Is it? It should be open." She tried the door. "That's weird. I know the girl that runs it, don't worry, let me text her. What's your name?"

"Ewen," I replied, extending a hand. "Nice to meet you."

"Hi Ewen. I'm Mary," she said with a beaming smile. "I'll just text her now. How come you're in Moron?" She glanced at my helmet. "You're here on a bike?"

"Yeah, that red one there." I pointed at Noddy, who was relaxing across the road. "I'm on my way to Bayan Olgii."

"Awesome! That's amazing!"

"Well, I might not make it on that. What do you do here? Are you visiting?"

"Oh, sort of, I work for the Peace Corps," Mary replied

with thick, syrupy r's. "I've been in Moron for about a year now."

"A year! That's a long time to spend out here. How have you found it?"

"Oh, I love it. It is hard at times, I mean you know, Mongolia isn't exactly the cleanest or the safest place and I miss home, but it's really great here. I'm moving now, which is why we've got all these boxes! But I'm hoping to stay in Mongolia for my next assignment."

A girl arrived. Mary welcomed her with an enthusiasm that I suspected was a personal trademark and explained what I was after. The girl (whose name I forgot to write in my notebook) knew a guesthouse run by a woman who was in contact with the herders. She agreed to ride on the back of Noddy to show me the way. I swapped numbers with Mary, left my pack in the tourist office and we rode back through Moron to a house behind a wall that was painted with a mural of reindeers grazing by a lakeside.

The girl introduced me to the owner, Saraa. She spoke excellent English and agreed to arrange for me to visit a family she knew in a few days' time. She also introduced me to her only other guest, a young English guy sitting on a thin mattress inside.

"Jimmy," he said as he stood. He had curly black hair and the beginnings of a beard.

"Ewen. How's things?"

"Yeah good man, good. Just editing some photos. What brings you here? That's your bike outside?"

"Yeah, that's mine." I glanced out the window. "I'm riding it to Olgii, but I thought I'd stop here and meet some herders."

"Ah, cool!" said Jimmy. "I'm doing something similar.

Except on a bicycle."

"On a bicycle? What?"

"Yeah. I wish I could have a motorcycle but I don't know how to ride one."

"But the distances! How long has it taken you?"

"A few months, so far." Jimmy scratched his head. "Takes ages to get anywhere!"

"I can imagine. What made you do it?"

"I'm making a documentary and trying to build a photography portfolio. I thought about going to uni, but this will give me some real experience, you know? Help build a profile."

"Wait a minute. How old are you?"

"Nineteen."

"Nineteen! Jesus. That's a hell of a lot more than I was doing at nineteen."

We spoke for a long time, both enjoying the first conversation in fluent English either of us had had for a while.

—

The following day, after getting Noddy a replacement clutch handle at a local mechanic, Jimmy and I set off to see some ancient standing stones he'd heard were nearby. I was keen to spend some time with someone other than myself. Jimmy was a bit nervous about riding on the back of Noddy. I reassured him that I was a cautious rider and wouldn't take any risks.

As we were on the road out of town, passing the spot I'd slept in when I arrived, I saw a young guy and a woman riding a motorcycle slowly across the grass towards the road on our right. The man turned his head towards us and we made brief eye contact. Noddy was cruising at about sixty kilometres an hour. I assumed he would slow down to let us pass and kept the throttle open, unconcerned.

He kept up his speed and shot out onto the road in front

of us.

There was nothing I could do to avoid a collision. Remarkably, I was able to process several thoughts as we hurtled towards the side of his heavy motorcycle. The first was that my trip was over. I was probably about to break a leg - most likely my right shin. Or was I about to become a paraplegic? Were these the last moments I'd have with functioning legs? I also had Jimmy behind me. He could break a bone too. To think I'd promised to ride carefully. Noddy was doomed. I wasn't going to cross Mongolia on a motorcycle after all. Was this really about to happen?

The heavy metal bars lining the side of the man's motorcycle loomed ominously. In a last-ditch effort, I threw my weight left and leaned Noddy at a sharp angle. We clipped their front tire with a loud crack, but miraculously stayed upright and came to a wobbly stop.

"Jesus, are you ok?" I turned to Jimmy.

"Yeah, I think so," he said shakily. "I banged my leg, but I think it's fine."

He dismounted gingerly and we had a look. He had a small cut on his shin and although it was sore and likely to bruise it was minor. My knee had clipped something but that too was fine.

"I'm so sorry Jimmy," I said. "I told you we wouldn't crash and here we are."

"No, no, it's ok, seriously" he reassured me. "You did an incredible job to avoid him. Just as long as we're both ok."

I looked at Noddy, fearing the worst. Incredibly, the only damage he'd suffered was a bent brake pedal and some cracked bodywork.

I breathed a sigh of relief and looked back down the road. The man's motorcycle was lying on its side and he was helping the woman stand up. I tensed. He saw us, I know he did, so why did he turn onto the road in front of us?

I stormed towards him with my arms held out in the 'what the hell was that?' position.

"Ok?" I asked, trying to suppress the anger. "Ok?"

He nodded. The woman was brushing dirt off her legs.

"Why did you pull out in front of me? You could've killed us!" I yelled suddenly.

"You!" he said back, pointing at my chest.

"As if it was me!" I spluttered. "I'm on the main road, you weren't even on the road, you can't just ride whenever you feel like!" I moved my hands into a T shape to motion my version of events.

He acquiesced. "Ok, ok, sorry. Sorry."

I calmed a little. I should've slowed down when I saw him coming. "It's ok. I'm sorry. Stupid, but we're all ok."

We helped him lift his bike and push it off the road. I gave him a ride back to his ger a few hundred metres away. After a quick visit to a mechanic to straighten Noddy's brake pedal with a crowbar, Jimmy and I back rode out to the stones.

They were about an hour away across a sandy plain and looked like a small graveyard lying just before the land rose into rocky hills. Each stone was roughly six feet tall with drawings of deer and weapons. Some showed men morphing into animals. I later discovered that they are known as deer stones and nobody knows what they were for. The most likely explanation is that they marked sites for rituals and sacrifices.

It was silent. There was no wind and no birds. Jimmy and I were the only people there. We took our time and walked slowly through the stones, calling to each other every so often to come and look at some strange drawing. Most were clear and sharp, as if they'd only been painted the week before.

It seemed strange to me that whoever made these stand, thousands of years ago, chose to put them here, at this random spot on a silent green plain. Yet the carved monoliths seemed almost familiar, like a folded corner in an old book, the only mark left by an unknown reader.

—

Jimmy left for Ulaanbaatar the next day, leaving me in Moron with not a lot to do. I had to wait for Saraa to get a special permit from the Mongolian military that would allow me to travel to the border with Russia. These permits used to be easy to acquire, but Saraa told me that people had strayed across the unmarked Russian border and had been shot at by Russian military patrols. Meanwhile, the Mongolian side had recently been plagued by bandits. This particular journey had the potential to be even more exciting than the hours I spent in a Thai war zone (although admittedly the bar was high).

Once the permit was ready Saraa drove me to the market to catch an overnight bus north to a village called Tsaaganuur. The bus was actually one of those old Soviet vans that look like a loaf of bread. It had eight seats, but fifteen of us were crammed in there with all our luggage, our knees intimately interlocking. I was bent slightly sideways over a box. We sat there for almost an hour, then drove in a short burst around Moron before returning to the same spot.

We waited a while longer. The driver got into another car and disappeared for half an hour, then returned and drove us to a nearby house with another van parked in front. It was loaded with cans of paint. We all got out and the driver and another man began loading the paint from the other van into ours.

I helped to speed up the process but was clueless about what was happening. Once half the paint cans were loaded the two spoke to each other for a minute, then began unloading the paint from our van and putting it back in the other one.

Three hours later we finally got underway (without any cans of paint). The van followed a paved road for a while before turning off onto the grass when the sun started to set. It then drove for twenty hours over the steppe, bouncing up and down and from side to side.

Sleep was impossible, so we all spent the time staring at each other. Well, the other passengers all stared at me and I alternated between staring at them and staring at the back of my eyelids.

The lady sitting across from me was chewing gum noisily. I toyed with the idea of putting her in a headlock and forcibly removing the gum with my fingers, then stared at the back of my eyelids some more.

At one point we stopped and met another bread loaf somewhere out on the endless grass. We unloaded half of the passengers and bags into the other loaf, drove twenty minutes in convoy and then piled everyone and everything back into the first loaf while the second drove off somewhere else. We trundled on through the darkness.

The sun rose to reveal an utterly different landscape. The rolling grasslands gave way to a lake, visible only as a thin silver line in the soft morning light, that was itself walled by an imposing line of white-capped mountains crested by an orange glow. The lady across from me had also stopped chewing gum. Hallelujah.

A few hours later we finally arrived in Tsaaganuur. It was a small, sparse, dusty village of wooden houses with colourful roofs spread along the lake's edge.

I unfolded myself off the box, glad to leave the loaf behind, and found the house that Saraa had told me to go to. A woman greeted me and lead me upstairs to a small bedroom, where I dropped my pack and changed my clothes before heading out for food.

When I returned an hour later I was greeted by two middle-aged American women. One was short and round, wearing an enormous necklace of carved reindeer antlers. She bustled about, followed attentively by the other, then stopped to speak to me.

They introduced themselves as anthropologists studying the local reindeer herders. Without so much as a hello, the short one started telling me off for bringing lollipops and cigarettes as gifts.

I stood silently, absorbing the tirade and catching apologetic glances from the woman's companion.

Once the anthropologist had finished she moved on to describing her work and handed me a business card. It advertised a company that "works to document life ways, lore and heart songs." I later used the card to clean my fingernails. I did, however, also go out to Tsaaganuur's only store to buy some pens and paper.

After a few hours a friendly-faced woman dressed in a purple deel walked in to the house.

"Hello! Anka," she said.

"Hi! I'm Ewen."

"Ewen. Hello! Come!"

I followed her out to a small car. A teenage boy sat in the driver's seat and two teenage girls sat in the back.

"Sovd," Anka said, pointing to the boy. He grinned at me.

Anka pointed at the girls. "Sumiya, Chitskey."

She then pointed at me. "Ewen."

We loaded my stuff into their car and drove out across the grass, following the course of a valley up into the hills. Sovd was driving.

"Sovd." Anka pointed at him, looked at me, then made a steering motion and held a thumbs-up. She then pointed at herself. "Anka." Thumbs down.

I laughed. "Ewen." I steered and made a thumbs-down. They laughed and Chitskey repeated my name before saying something in their language.

The conversation continued that way until, an hour or two later, we stopped at the edge of a thick pine forest right at the end of the valley. A small boy, no more than six or seven years old, came trotting out of the woods on the back of a reindeer with four others in tow. I stared.

Anka turned to me and pointed at the reindeer.

"Tsaa," she said. "Tsaa."

"Ah," I replied. "Tsaa." Sovd laughed.

They loaded the reindeer with luggage and helped me mount up. My feet were brushing the ground, but the animal took my weight without complaint. The girls giggled at me wobbling uncertainly as we trotted off into the forest.

Reindeer are actually surprisingly easy to ride. Easier than horses, in my limited experience of both. Although they're small, so small, and I was often worried mine would slip under my weight but it never did, even across streams and thick mud.

We climbed steadily into the hills. The trees around us were scraggly, weather-beaten things, but a subtle hint of green showed spring was almost here. The ground underneath the reindeer's splayed hooves changed from pine needles to bog and then to soft moss. The animal's legs made a soft clicking noise while we trotted along, like sparks on a gas stovetop, and its furry antlers rose up and down rhythmically.

Eventually we emerged from a thicket of trees and there, in front of me, were teepees and a wooden pen full of reindeer, set amidst the forest.

—

The Tsaatan, which literally translates as 'reindeer people', live a nomadic life in 100,000 square kilometres of taiga forest straddling the Russian-Mongolian border. They are, culturally speaking, the forefathers of Native Americans – hence the teepees, which they call 'ortz'. While we tied up the reindeer Anka introduced me to her husband Magsar, a small, wiry guy with a face weathered by the wind and crinkled by laugh lines.

Together they showed me into their ortz. It was small, no more than three metres in diameter and the same high, but wasn't lacking for equipment. They had a satellite television, a phone, almost everything except a computer and internet. Low beds ringed the edge of the ortz, facing a TV and a small carpet at the back. A wood-burning stove and chimney sat in the middle. The walls were made of branches leaning towards a central opening at the top in typical teepee style, all wrapped in a grey canvas. The floor was made of thicker branches cut into shape and laid in lines.

Anka showed me where to drop my pack and offered me tea. We began the slow process of learning to communicate.

"Bi," Anka said, pointing at herself. "Chi." She pointed at me. I repeated the words and gestures. They laughed and nodded.

"Bi, Mongo," Magsar said and gestured around us. "Mongo. Chi?"

"Bi... Australia?" I tried. They looked at me, confused.

"England?" I tried again.

"Angli!" Magsar cried. "Chi Angli!" He pointed at Anka. "Anka, Heej Magsar." I repeated the word. Wife.

He pointed at Chitskey, who was watching the process with amusement. "Chitskey, Hoo."

I repeated again and pointed at Sovd. "Sovd, Hoo."

Magsar nodded and pointed at himself. "Bi, Magsar. Sovd, Chitskey, Hoo." Child. "Anka, Heej."

I was getting it. "Anka, Heej. Marska, Anka, Sovd, Chitskey, all Tsaatan."

They all burst out laughing. "Tsaatan," Magsar said. "Tsaatan."

Through this process I slowly learned that Magsar and Anka had four sons and a daughter. The two oldest sons, whose names I never learnt, were followed by Sovd and Chitskey (who I think were twins) and a younger brother named Molkch. The family shared the camp with another living in a second ortz further into the forest. The second family had three children; Sumiya, a young girl of no more than six named Shingei, and a young boy. The names came fast and it took a number of attempts to write some down, although I couldn't get all of them.

Magsar was a joker, loud and constantly laughing at my attempts to learn Tsaatan. Anka tolerated his boisterousness with a smile and went to great lengths to make sure I was comfortable, constantly offering me tea (which was really just hot milk) and little bread biscuits. Sovd was shy at first, but open, although the oldest boys were distant and largely ignored my presence. The young ones took a great interest in me, especially Shingei and showed particular interest in my iPad. The older girls, Chitskey and Sumiya, were also curious about this solitary newcomer with the ginger beard, although they soon left the ortz to talk between themselves.

After I'd learnt some elementary Tsaatan Sovd and the oldest boys left to make some firewood. I saw an opportunity to get to know them and help out a little. They sat next to a pile of tree limbs near the ortz and watched me silently when I joined them. Sovd spoke to the others, who laughed and beckoned to me. They pointed to a particularly large limb lying on the ground nearby and mimed picking it up.

"Where do you want it?" I asked, pointing at the pile. Sovd nodded.

I bent down and tried to lift the limb, which was far heavier than I thought. The boys laughed while I struggled visibly. I managed to lever it onto my shoulder and took a break.

"Heavy!" I exclaimed, patting the wood. They remained silent and looked at me expectantly.

I bent my legs, took the weight of the log and tried lift it off the ground. For a moment I thought it would crush me, but the fear of embarrassment was a powerful motivator. I pushed upwards with a grunt, moved a few steps forward and dropped it on the pile with a loud thump.

The boys laughed and clapped my back, suddenly open and welcoming. "Angli!"

I spent much of the first day playing games with the youngest children around the camp. They were easily pleased and were soon begging to be picked up and swung in circles. Anka eventually sheltered me from their attention in the ortz and taught me more of their language over hot tea.

As night finally fell Anka showed me my bed - a narrow wooden shelf on the edge of the ortz made of tree branches covered in blankets. I lifted all the blankets up and lay on the wood. This prompted a lot of laughter from the assembled family. Magsar, who was sitting cross-legged in his traditional position at the head of the ortz, indicated that the bottom blanket was the mattress. Now imagine that you had an exchange student staying at your house and when you showed them to their room, they lifted up the entire mattress and tucked themselves underneath, straight on the bed slats. That is what I did.

The night was short. Because we were so far north the

light didn't fade until midnight, and even then left a smear on the horizon until the sun poked through the trees a few hours later. At least five of us packed into the ortz to sleep, so there was no privacy. Magsar and Anka shared a bed not much wider than me. Sovd and Chitskey shared another, with their heads almost touching their parent's feet. I had a bed to myself on the other side of the ortz and the three smallest children shared a tiny bed at the head of mine. I woke up several times throughout the night with my head sandwiched between the heads of two sleeping children and was woken a few more times by sudden kicks in the face when they changed positions or twitched in their sleep.

—

And so, without speaking a word of each other's languages, I settled in comfortably with Magsar and Anka's family. The days revolved entirely around the reindeer. The men would wake at six to take the herd out into the taiga to feed. Anka would rise later to prepare food, wash clothes and chat on the satellite phone.

When Magsar returned in the late morning we'd split the reindeer into three groups; calves were tied to tree roots with their mothers hobbled nearby, males and young females were kept in the pen and a few reindeer that could be ridden were tied near the ortz. We'd then have lunch together in the ortz, which was either hot soup with boiled reindeer meat or cold reindeer milk with mysterious floating white chunks.

The afternoons were lazy. Some of the adults would nap while the kids and I ran around playing hide and seek. Sometimes I'd read my book, lying on the soft moss near Magsar as he carved reindeer antlers into small trinkets that he'd eventually sell in town for a small bit of cash.

Magsar and I talked while we sat. Through many hand gestures I learnt that the kids were on holiday and normally attended a school in Tsaaganuur in the winter. When the snows came, Magsar and Sovd would leave the family for a few months and take the reindeer three hundred kilometres north, following the moss. The moss, he said, was everything.

Magsar also took to sneaking up behind me when I was reading and blowing on the back of my neck, which never failed to scare me. I did the same back and soon both of us were sneaking around the camp, constantly on our guard.

In the late afternoon Magsar would take the reindeer into the taiga again and return around ten for dinner.

One night, while we were sleeping, the dogs kicked up an absolute racket at about three in the morning. I woke with a start and lay still. There was a scuffling noise outside and more ferocious barking, followed shortly thereafter by a bone-chilling howl.

Everyone sat bolt upright. My blood ran cold. Magsar jumped up with a speed that defied his age, grabbed an old rifle lying near his bed and rushed outside. He made an enormous booming noise from deep in his chest, like a clap of thunder or a fighter jet breaking the sound barrier. It was a mighty, almost inhuman, and it echoed through the forest. The dogs quietened.

The next morning I brought it up as we ate breakfast. "Many wolves?" I asked, holding up a number of fingers. He nodded.

"Many," he replied with a sweep of his arm. "Many many. Taiga, many."

—

Soon Magsar felt comfortable enough with my riding skills to take me herding, so one evening we saddled up two reindeer and padded off into the taiga, leading the herd behind us. Magsar went ahead and deftly steered his reindeer through the spongy moss. He was wrapped in a thick black robe that was covered in tufts of white fur and held a smooth wooden staff. He looked like a wizard out of a children's book.

Together we guided the herd through the forest. It was silent, save for the clicks of the reindeer, the occasional chirp of a bird and the ever-present sound of water. Small streams gurgled and bubbled all around us, disappearing into their hidden pathways through the soft moss and reappearing in tiny waterfalls that babbled happily into clear pools.

The land began to rise. After climbing for an hour or so we came to the crest of a hill. Magsar stopped his reindeer at the top and leant on his staff, beckoning me.

As I rode up the scraggly forest suddenly gave way. Rolling forested hills and grassy valleys rippled outwards towards a distant ring of snow-capped mountains, and to the north the forest ceded to a forbidding expanse of what seemed to be white, ice-covered tundra. It was the sort of landscape that could hide a dragon. There was nothing human in sight, no roads, no power lines, no distant dwelling. The rain giants were marching again, hiding the land behind each grey stride.

Magsar and I sat on a rocky outcrop, silently overlooking the view as the reindeer munched nearby. I could do nothing but gaze at the world beneath our feet.

At the time, some small part of me was aware that this was the climax of my story. Of all the places I'd seen - the empty Nullarbor, the vast Indian Ocean, the tea plantations of highland Malaysia and the dusty plains of Bagan, through dark caves and towering cities and the cold majesty of the Great Wall - I knew this would appear first in my memories, this time I spent in a primal land ruled by a wizard and his reindeer.

"Russki," Magsar said, pointing west. Russia.

He then tapped my chest and pretended to tie a ponytail behind his head. "Chi, Heej?"

I nodded. "In Australia."

"Chi, Ee-wen. Bi, Magsar. Heej?"

"Heej Danika."

"Dah-neeka." He patted the rock underneath us. "Dahneeka, Mongo?"

I laughed and shook my head. "Too cold for her, I think." I shivered to demonstrate.

Magsar chuckled, then pointed at me and drew a tear line down his cheek.

I nodded again.

He patted my shoulder. "Chi, Angli, Heej, Hoo, Mongo." He mimed going and returning.

"I come back with Danika?" I asked, accompanying the words with gestures.

"Chi, Heej, Hoo," he replied. Child.

"Bi, Heej, Hoo, come to see Tsataan," I said, pointing at myself and at him.

He nodded and grinned, then looked at the view one last time. His eyes seemed to miss nothing as they swept over the expanse, gauging which way the giants marched. It truly was another world, similar and yet so different - so remarkably unchanged.

"Ya wee!" Magsar cried, suddenly jumping to his feet. Let's go!

—

Soon it was my last night on the taiga. Magsar assembled the family and we went to the other ortz for dinner. When we ducked under the low entrance, Magsar instructed me to sit on a reindeer skin at the head of the ortz. This was normally reserved for the husband, who smiled at me and sat on my left. Magsar sat on my right and the two families formed a silent ring around the edge of the ortz.

Magsar extended his hands and presented a carved bit of antler in the shape of a reindeer, strung on a length of homemade leather. It meant a lot. To carve the antlers he used a saw made from a short length of thin, fraying steel cable strung across a curved bone. He had no extra cable and the place to buy more was in Ulaanbaatar - an impossible distance for him.

Anka smiled at me as Magsar leaned forward to tie the cord around my neck. After he leant back, she walked forward and presented me with a hard block of white cheese, made from reindeer milk.

"Heet heet, moto," she said, miming me eating the cheese on the motorcycle.

"Bayarla, Anka, bayarla." I thanked her with a smile.

Magsar straightened up and clasped my forearm with a powerful grip. "You, good man." It was the first time he'd spoken any English.

"Thank you, Magsar," I replied, grasping his forearm in return. "As are you." I looked at Anka. "Thank you. Bayarla." I wished I had something to give them, but other than cash and the gifts I'd brought, words were all I had.

Magsar strengthened his grip and looked at me. The fire flickered in the centre of the ortz. "Chi, Tsaatan."

11
THE MOUNTAINS

I returned to Saraa's guesthouse in Moron on another cramped overnight bread loaf across the steppe. I spent a day with her husband, a tall, serious military man in uniform who had recently returned from a border patrol. He had a good look at Noddy and found a wobbly wheel that I hadn't noticed, so took me to the local markets to get some new parts.

I found some Internet and received a message from Jean, who had attempted the northern route while I was staying in the taiga. The road was impassable, he said, blocked by swollen rivers carrying spring meltwater. He had attempted to ford one and nearly lost his bike. It was dragged out of the water by a truck. Jean was far more experienced than I was. If he couldn't do it, Noddy and I stood no chance.

As Saraa's husband and I were putting the finishing touches on the wheel I fetched my map and asked him about the northern road. He shook his head.

"No, no good." He pointed at a village named Tsagaan Uul, about a hundred kilometres west of Moron, then traced his finger another hundred kilometres south, then west again.

"Better," he said. "Tsagaan Uul, Tosontsengel, Ulaangom. Ulaangom Olgii, I don't know. Many mountains."

"So better to go south for now," I confirmed, pointing at the names on my map. "First to Tsagaan Uul, then to Tosontsengel, then to Ulaangom."

He nodded. "Road good for..." He mimed a big steering wheel.

"The road is for trucks?"

"Yes. Possible with bike." He patted Noddy.

"And through the mountains?"

He shrugged. "Must ask in Ulaangom."

And so my route was decided. I would follow the northern route for a day, then head south and skirt the edge of the Gobi Desert across the country. Beyond that lay the Altai - over four and a half thousand metres of skyward rock that I did not yet know how to cross. But that was not today's problem.

—

I stocked up on water and petrol and set off early the next morning. I rode fast and eager at first and had to force myself to slow down. The taiga was my last detour. From here I was heading straight to Switzerland by any means necessary. Home lay far over that western horizon, past the one beyond that and through countless horizons - but home is where I was finally going.

Yet Olgii was only the first step, and that was well over another thousand kilometres across Mongolia. This time there was no road.

Not far out of Moron the tarmac stopped. I followed dirt tracks across the grass. There were dozens wandering in all directions, making it difficult to tell which to follow. I followed the largest and kept the sun on my left in the hope it was heading to where I wanted to be. I used my phone as a makeshift GPS and checked it every so often to confirm my bearings.

The tracks followed a river for a while through green valleys flanked by muscular hills. There were few other travellers on the road and soon I was entirely alone. The remoteness of Mongolia loomed like a shadow. A breakdown here would mean waiting hours for someone to come by. A fall or an injury would be far worse.

I passed a flock of enormous black vultures perched on an isolated rock formation rising out of the steppe. They watched me silently, turning their bald heads as Noddy buzzed along like an enthusiastic little lawn mower.

The valleys eventually gave way to rolling grasslands. Fluffy white clouds lay low in a blue sky, close enough to touch. I came to a fork in the track and decided to head right.

As the sun hung high in the sky I passed a horseman watching over his herd. He waved me over for a brief hello and pointed at Noddy, giving me a thumbs-up. I returned the gesture.

"Tsagaan Uul?" I asked, pointing over the low hills in front. It was the first time I'd spoken all day. My voice was dry and harsh. We were alone on a green sea.

He nodded. "Tsagaan Uul, Tsagaan Uul."

Shortly afterwards I came across a convoy of trucks parked on the side of the dirt track for repairs. The drivers waved me over. They were a friendly group and took turns sitting on Noddy and wearing my helmet. We took a few photos together before I set off again.

After another two hours I crested a hill and saw a sparkling blue lake in the middle of the rolling grass, bordered by a little village. I sighed with relief and made my way slowly towards the promise of petrol.

I refuelled at the village's only pump and sat back on Noddy, ready to find somewhere to set up camp. I pulled the clutch handle and pressed the ignition switch. Nothing happened. Not again, please. I tried a second time. Nothing. I was attracting the attention of a few local men standing nearby. I shifted gears to neutral and pressed the switch. Noddy coughed back to life.

One guy offered to have a look. I switched off, dismounted and let him on. He tried starting Noddy with the clutch handle pulled in, but also had no luck. He shrugged and dismounted. I thanked him anyway, turned Noddy on through neutral and rode far out of town to pitch my tent on a hillside overlooking the lake. I wasn't in the mood for another surprise foot massage.

The lake glittered a soft gold in the early sunlight and letting off small wisps of fog. After a morning coffee we set off again, this time heading south. Noddy's clutch handle was still acting up, but at least there was still a way to turn him on and move forward.

The track, however, quickly led into dry marshlands and disappeared. I stood on Noddy's pedals as I rode to try and find it again, but it was nowhere to be seen. Two horsemen watched me from the dryer grass on the far side. I rode towards them. Their horses skitted nervously when I approached.

"Sainbainuu," I said, removing my helmet. They watched me silently.

"Tosontsengel?" I asked. The younger man pointed to the hills behind him while the other stuck a finger deep into an ear to scratch an itch.

"Bayarla," I said. Thank you. He nodded.

I rode into the hills and discovered a southward track. Wide tire marks were evident in the dirt, probably left by a truck. This must be the right road.

I followed it, staring at Noddy's front wheel as I carefully chose a path between the rocks embedded in the ground. Groves of pine trees began to quietly crowd around us and the sunlight strengthened.

I soon found the trucks themselves parked at the bottom of a small decline, next to a trickling stream that lost itself in a muddy bog. One truck was leaning heavily to the right with its front wheel almost completely swallowed by the mud. One driver was tending a small fire while the others squatted around the wheel.

I stopped on the top of the incline to pick a path, then stood on the pedals and rode Noddy across the mud, slightly upstream from the trucks. They watched and shook their heads when we floated straight across. I patted Noddy's fuel tank affectionately. It was a good thing I could only afford a small bike. This would've been much harder if he was any heavier.

I followed the dirt strips for an hour as they lead into a dark forest and slowly petered out in boggy, mossy ground. Where was the track? This can't be the right way. I couldn't afford to be lost for long with Noddy's tiny fuel tank. Worried, I stopped and checked my phone. A white line lay some way west of where my little blue arrow was. Maybe that was a road. The trees were silent and pressed in closer, watching us with dark eyes.

Noddy and I pressed on. The forest seemed to lead us along paths of its own. We crossed small, bubbling streams and muscled through bogs of thick mud that spattered up my thighs. Please, I thought, please let that white line be a road.

The forest eventually gave up and drew back to reveal a flat green plain so vast that it faded into an indeterminate blue. I could just make out some tiny white dots in the distance, probably gers, and made a mental note of where they were.

As the mud gave way to dry grass I saw, to my immense relief, two faint lines heading west. I whooped excitedly inside my helmet and opened the throttle. Noddy surged forward, mirroring my eagerness, and we flew across the steppe.

At midday I finally saw two dust plumes far in the distance and headed towards them. The dust was rising from two vans following a well-worn, wide strip of dirt running north to south. This, I assumed, was the route to Tosontsengel. I whooped excitedly and awarded myself some slices of salami and Anka's cheese to celebrate.

That route, however, wasn't much better. While the tracks climbed southwards the grass became progressively sandier, and sand is hell on a motorcycle. Noddy frequently slipped sideways and forced me to drop a foot to the ground to keep us upright. Even at slow speeds, each impact jarred through my knees and hips as if someone were swinging a wrecking ball into the bottom of my boots. Soon I was swearing aloud. Every ten metres was an exhausting mental and physical effort. I silently kept going, trying to turn anger into forward motion. I listened to some motivating music for as long as I could tolerate the pain of wearing earbuds inside a tight-fitting helmet. The silence returned.

The land dried and became rockier as we moved south. Low hills rose and became a serrated rocky range that walled us into barren, dusty brown valleys. The track ran alongside a power line, reassuring me that we were heading the right direction, but progress slowed even further. Lengthening stretches of shifting sand tried to topple us over and sharp rocks chewed the soft rubber of Noddy's wheels. Eagles soared far overhead while we moved slowly through their valleys, turning in high lazy circles on invisible currents.

After hours of painfully slow riding, the valley opened into another wide green plain bisected by numerous tracks heading west. I saw a group of trucks parked next to a solitary brick building and pulled up. They belonged to the same group of drivers I'd met the day before, who were eating lunch inside.

They welcomed me to their table, and after spending some time admiring my beard they told me they were going to Ulaangom and offered to travel together.

We set off in convoy, passing by the edge of a lake made grey by the thickening clouds overhead. A light rain began to sprinkle down.

In the late afternoon Noddy chugged to a stop. He was out of fuel. I emptied the emergency jerry can into his tank and rode after the trucks, but he slipped and skidded on the thick sand and hammered my legs on the ground. The rain came down harder. It sounded as if someone was pouring rice on top of my helmet. I looked at the truck drivers, dry in their cabins and driving on four wheels.

In the early evening we passed through a small village. The trucks pressed on while I stopped to refuel. I set off again soon after, relieved that the rain had stopped. I was getting in a good rhythm and marvelled at the land around as we rode, with its shifting moods and vast, empty expanses.

The trucks' tire marks wobbled across a flat grassland then disappeared in some foothills. These offered a good place to set up camp. I began to dream of the steaming pot of instant noodles I was about to enjoy.

Noddy, however, had other plans. Just when I was about to stop for the night we hit some thick sand in a sunken section of track and he toppled over, throwing me hard onto the ground and dropping his weight onto my left leg. I slammed into the embankment and lay there for a moment, struggling to breathe.

I groaned. Just a moment ago I was cruising along, making steady westward progress and now I was lying on the ground, alone and with a leg trapped underneath well over twice my bodyweight's worth of machine and luggage.

A thought then sprang to mind. I leant forward to check the clutch handle. It was fine. Phew.

A pair of headlights flashed in the distance, about a kilometre from where I lay. I ripped my helmet off and yelled and waved, but I was hidden in the sunken track and the lights passed by unawares.

I then stared at the darkening sky. The stars were emerging one by one, as if someone was poking little pinholes in a deep blue blanket. I was far from any sort of settlement, darkness was falling and there was no guarantee a vehicle would pass this way again, and if one did, that it would even see me in the growing gloom.

"Oh, fuck," I whispered. The steppe watched me with merciless indifference.

I tried lifting Noddy, heaving as hard as I could, but I was lying on my side and had no leverage. I gave another heave and he budged a little before settling his weight back onto my leg. Some knob on the engine dug painfully into my calf.

I leaned forward to undo my pack off the back, but decided that would be an even greater inconvenience so I lifted again with every last fibre I could find, crying aloud with the effort. He moved slightly and after another big push I pulled my leg free. It was sore but uninjured.

I then righted Noddy and tried to turn him on, but of course he didn't feel like going anywhere and simply let off a series of lazy clicks. I looked around and saw some smoke drifting skywards from over a small rise about a kilometre away. There was no other choice. I abandoned Noddy and started walking.

Darkness had almost completely fallen when I approached the camp. A fire crackled in the middle of several trucks and a large tent, casting flickering shadows. It was the only light on the steppe.

Three enormous dogs heard my footsteps and ran towards me, growling and barking viciously. I stopped and waited as they bounded over, tensing reflexively when they covered the last few metres and sniffed at me, growling softly with exposed fangs. A young guy followed them.

"Sanbainuu," I called out.

He stopped at the sudden sound, then approached me slowly, suspicious of a man emerging out of the darkness in the middle of nowhere. "Sanbainuu."

I mimed a motorcycle falling over and pointed behind me. He looked into the darkness, then called back towards the firelight. Two more men walked over.

"Sanbainuu," I said again.

"Sanbainuu," one replied. He was significantly older than the others. "English?"

"Yes," I said in a wave of relief. "I fell off my motorcycle and it won't start. It's somewhere out there."

He looked into the darkness, then turned to the others and gave a few instructions. "Wait here," he said before turning on his heel back to the camp.

The three returned moments later in a four-wheel drive and beckoned for me to sit in the front. Noddy quickly appeared in the headlights and one of the men jumped out. It only took him a few moments to realize that the problem was a loose spark plug. Noddy spluttered back to life indignantly.

"Thanks so much,' I said, shaking their hands. I could've hugged them.

"Where are you going?" the older guy asked.

"Ulaangom," I replied, "although no further now."

He nodded. "Come with us. Too dark to go further today."

We returned to their camp and I was shown a spot to pitch my tent, which I did with the last of the light before returning to the campfire. One guy was cooking thin legs of meat over the hissing fire while five others sat around some boxes. The English-speaking man sat at the head of the group.

"So, you go to Ulaangom."

"Yes, and then to Olgii," I said. "From there I will go to Russia, after I decide what to do with that bike."

"Mm," he looked at the fire thoughtfully. "You must be careful in Russia. I studied there, in Novosibirsk. Russia is very dangerous."

"I'm not planning on staying there too long. What did you study in Novosibirsk?"

"Economics. I was in Novosibirsk for three years." He leaned forward and grabbed a leg of meat, then cut strips off it with a machete. The blade scraped on the bone.

Another man offered me a knee joint. I accepted and snapped in half to make it more manageable. The men all cheered and the leader leaned over and clapped me on the shoulder. The sudden gesture took me by surprise.

"You are a man!" he said. "Big beard, tough hands. A man. You Western men get meat, fondle it with soft fingers. Not you, you are strong. Alone on a motorcycle, eating meat. This is good in Mongolia. People like you. Mongolian men are strong!" He translated for the others, who nodded in agreement while they hacked tough meat off the large bones with shining machetes.

I was reminded of the boys on the taiga and their strange test with the tree. It all seemed a bit insecure to me, but I kept that thought to myself as I watched the men scrape the machetes expertly along the bones as if they were sharpening the blades.

"What are you doing out here?" I asked as I peeled leathery meat apart with cold fingers. The fire crackled and sent a column of sparks into the clear night sky. The darkness swallowed the sparks in a quick rebuke.

"Laying cable," the man replied as he poured vodka

into a plastic cup. "Fibre."

He pushed the cup towards me and pointed to a digger parked on the steppe, just visible at the edge of the firelight. "From Ulaangom to Ulaanbaatar."

"That's a long way. How long will it take?" I said through a mouthful of meat.

"Yes, long way. We have already been out here three weeks. But I like the country. It is clean. Good for the lungs."

I agreed with that and downed the vodka. It burned.

We spoke a while longer, mostly about my trip, Mongolia, and fibre optic cable. Eventually the leader stood and yawned. The others immediately stood.

"I sleep," he said. "Sleep in the big tent. But your tent, your tent is very small."

I shrugged. "It is, but it fits me and all my stuff."

"But what do you do about the wolves?"

I looked at him, then glanced into the darkness beyond. "The wolves? I don't know. What do you do about them?"

He translated for the others, who laughed and pointed at the trucks. "We sleep in the trucks," he said. "You only have this little tent? This is crazy."

"I guess I sleep with this." I pulled out my little pocketknife. The man burst into laughter along with the others, holding his belly and leaning backwards.

"With that?" he asked, wiping his eyes. "No, no. Tonight you sleep with this." He handed me his machete. "Keep it close!"

"I didn't know there were wolves this far south," I said.

"There are wolves everywhere in Mongolia. Here especially, many wolves. They come from miles, smell the meat. If they smell food they will rip into your tent." He clapped me forcefully on the back. "Good luck! Hopefully we see you in the morning!"

After a tense but uneventful night I woke early with the men, sipping hot coffee and clasping the mug close to my chest to try and steal some heat. The dawn revealed that we were in a narrow pass through the hills that opened onto an expanse of sand and dust.

Once the coffee was gone I thanked the men again and packed Noddy.

"Remember, be very careful in Russia," the leader said as I put my helmet on. It seemed an odd thing to say, coming from a guy wielding a machete in the wilds of western Mongolia, but I took it to heart. "Very dangerous, Russia."

I nodded and thanked him one last time. I could feel them watching while Noddy and I wobbled off, unsteady on the sand.

The day passed much the same as the last. We passed over more sand, washboard gravel and rocky plains. The views, however, were spectacular. Angry storm clouds brewed over sharp red hills as we weaved our way along and blue lakes stretched wide amidst a sea of grass that shimmered restlessly in the wind. I stopped frequently to admire the view and watch the weather roll overhead. I had no cares. The only plan I had to make was how to reach the far edge of this green and empty world.

One of the unfortunate downsides to this open landscape, however, was that there was nowhere secluded to poo. The only option was to head far enough off the track so that, in the unlikely event someone happened past, they'd be unable to make out the exact details. After a coffee break I grabbed my roll of toilet paper and found a secluded spot off the track.

Midway through I was interrupted by a surprisingly loud neigh from behind me. Startled, I rotated my head as far as I could and saw a herder on a horse staring at me.

I was literally caught with my pants around my ankles. He couldn't have appeared at a worse time. The man had a look on his face like he'd just seen a ghost. I suppose I'd be equally surprised if I was on a walk in my neighbourhood and stumbled across a Mongolian nomad lifting up his blue deel and shitting on the footpath.

I waved and turned back around, groaning inwardly. There was nothing for it but to continue under the silent scrutiny of some dude on a horse. After I was done I said a quick hello and walked briskly back to Noddy.

The herder, however, followed and dismounted to get a better look at the bike. He patted the seat and smiled, giving me a thumbs-up. I smiled back, thinking about the fact that we'd known each other for five minutes and he'd already seen more of me than I have. Of course the first person I'd encountered in hours had stumbled upon me mid-poo. Typical.

Noddy and I continued. After a few hours we came to a small cluster of shacks in the middle of the vastness. This was the last opportunity to fill the tank for more than 250 kilometres, leaving me with only thirty kilometres of spare fuel (including my emergency reserve). I was following tracks and using the sun as rough compass, and like I'd previously discovered, one wrong decision could lead to hours lost on the steppe. The margin of error was small.

I filled Noddy's tank and was approached by a man who I presumed would take payment. I tapped the jerry can strapped on the rack.

"For benzene?" I asked hopefully, then pointed at a small brick building nearby that I assumed was a store.

He looked at the can and shook his head. I pulled out my map and showed him the next settlement, then patted Noddy's fuel tank and shook my head. He thought for a moment, walked over to the brick building and returned with a bottle of Sprite.

"Bayarla," I said, handing him money. I emptied the bottle on the ground and filled it with petrol. It only gave me two extra litres, but it would have to do.

—

I rode on. The grass thinned into red dust and the hills became barren. This was the northernmost edge of the Gobi, the frontier between steppe and desert. Riding became easier on the firm ground, although the track had corrugated over time and rattled Noddy violently, forcing me to slow dramatically. Soon the land flattened completely, interrupted only by outcrops of red rock emerging suddenly from the yellow-brown sand.

The corrugated track began to really test my patience. There was no escape, no smoother route other than the one that shook us violently no matter how slow I went, shaking all of Noddy's loose parts in a constant rattle of plastic and thumping my spine down, down, down against the seat. The frustration grew and I roared inside my helmet in an attempt to let off some steam. I put my headphones back in and was able to tolerate them for about half an hour before my ears became too sore. The rattling continued.

In the afternoon we came across some bulldozers and a raised dirt road across the grass. It appeared to be the first stage of a real highway. Desperate for firmer ground, I dismounted Noddy and climbed up the road's steep banks of loose earth. The road itself wasn't paved but it was smoother than the corrugated tracks.

I spent ten minutes digging a path up the bank, then

rode Noddy up and on. We spent the rest of the day following this road. It was blocked every kilometre or so by huge mounds of earth that forced me to dismount and dig a path through for Noddy, but even this was better than the endless rattling.

In the early evening the road suddenly became asphalt. I couldn't believe it. A paved road!

I stopped, switched Noddy off and lay on the surface. I'd never experienced anything so smooth in all my life. I felt the heat of the road through my hands. What a wonderful thing, I thought, this asphalt. Absolutely humanity's greatest creation. I celebrated with some slices of salami and a chunk of Anka's cheese before riding on, hitting sixty kilometres an hour for the first time since leaving Ulaanbaatar. An ominous storm front was forming to the north, creating a dance of light and dark on the hills underneath a deep blue that spoke of rain.

A lake soon emerged on my left, pulling in a strong wind that made Noddy wobble in the gusts. A herd of camels raised their heads curiously when I pulled over to fill up. Their thick red winter wool was peeling off and looked as if they were wearing a ragged old blanket flung carelessly over their humps. They watched, chewing nonchalantly while I emptied the Sprite bottle into Noddy's tank. Drops of petrol splattered over my jeans in the gusting wind and spread dark splotches among the existing grease stains.

I reached a small settlement late that evening and gladly refuelled before setting up camp a few kilometres away, on the edge of a dry lake. As I hammered in the last tent peg, my eyes caught a burst of sudden colour. I straightened and looked around. A rainbow speared downwards onto the red lakebed, painted by the last rays of dying light, while behind me the sun was busy setting the sky on fire above a dark wall of brooding mountains, their white peaks blending into the clouds above.

I stood, stunned. It was almost as if I was in a land that time had flown over and forgotten - one of the few places I'd ever been that was so primal, so untamed, like I was standing alone in a pen with a bear grunting and pacing on powerful legs back and forth and back and forth before stopping, unexpectedly, to stare back at me with orange eyes.

—

I woke early and unzipped the tent to see the lakebed again, soft and welcoming. The wall of mountains loomed to the west.

I had two options. The first was to head to Ulaangom, a morning's ride north, to see if I could find someone who knew a route through the mountains. The second was to turn south again and ride a few hundred kilometres to the city of Khovd, which lay on the main road between Ulaanbaatar and Bayan Olgii. It was spring, meaning most mountain roads were probably blocked by swollen rivers. The main road was open year-round. It was a significant detour, but it was the safe option.

I packed up, strapped my stuff onto Noddy and pressed the ignition. Nothing happened. I sighed and tried again. Nothing. I looked around. There was a ger a few kilometres away and I wasn't too far from a settlement, but I decided to try and hill-start him first.

I unloaded my stuff and pushed Noddy up a small rise by the lake. He was heavy. I leaned into the handlebars and pushed against the earth, utterly breathless after a few metres. My thighs burned with the effort. Once I thought we had enough height I got on and rode him down the hill, letting the clutch handle out and pressing the ignition. Nothing happened.

I turned him around and stared at the incline for a moment before heaving him back up the hill, grunting under the strain. I stopped and sat at the top to catch my breath. The lakebed bathed in the dawn light, hiding shy behind small strips of wispy fog. I rode him down the hill again but nothing happened. Fighting a sinking sensation, I gave Noddy another look-over and realized that I hadn't reset the kill switch, which I'd used to turn him off the night before. I muttered some sarcasm his way when he wheezed back to life.

I rode along the paved highway for a bit longer before turning off onto rocky ground to follow a power line south. The land became drier and hotter as I went on and much steeper.

The tracks curved up hills and onto small plateaus before dropping again onto the most barren, rocky plain I'd yet encountered. It was the colour of slate, nothing but sharp rocks and triangular outcrops under a beating sun, with not even a memory of water. I stopped to survey the view, then descended.

The tracks I was following became unreadable. I checked my phone. There was no signal. All I could do was use the sun to confirm that the wobbly powerline was still leading me south. The rocks were serrated and menacing and snapped at Noddy's tires while I twisted the handlebars left and right to avoid them, left, right, over and over, again and again. I swore again inside my helmet, cursing the rocks and the goddamn sand, trying in vain to break a deafening silence that seemed to tell me off as it effortlessly swallowed the sound of my voice.

The rocks became so sharp and unsteady that I had to stop and push Noddy, afraid I'd puncture a tire or fall again. If either of those things happened, the water bottles in my pack would become an hourglass. There were no gers nearby, no passing travellers, nobody but me and this motorcycle. Everything hung on whether those old, cracked, worn tires would survive for long enough to get me past this Martian plain.

Noddy, for once, didn't let me down. We passed through and after innumerable hours finally happened across a small village. I refuelled and bought some sort of packaged cake from the only store to give me something to look forward to before pushing on through the sun-baked desert, crawling along under a cloudless sky.

The sand stretched away to my left throughout the afternoon, orange and flat as paper save for a single solitary, lonely mountain. It had no place being there, rising from the sand all by itself, thrusting up a defiant peak that created its own clouds. I stopped to take a photo. A herd of camels were the only other sign of life.

I arrived in Khovd when the sun was dropping, dusty, thirsty and tired. It was a fairly large town, the largest I'd seen since Moron. I refuelled and parked outside a small brick shack with a Coca-Cola sign hanging out front. The inside was dark and empty, but a few tables were arrayed in front of a kitchen. This must be a place to eat.

An old woman with ragged white hair appeared through a doorway and looked at me.

"Sanbainuu," I said, then mimed a knife and fork.

She continued to stare at me. I mimed again and said what I thought was the Mongolian word for eating. "Heet heet?"

She remained confused. I picked up a menu lying on the table and pointed at an item, then mimed again. Surely this was a restaurant? Why else would there be menus on the tables?

She still seemed confused and stared at me. I sat down, unsure what else I could say, then pointed at the menu again. She nodded and shuffled back through the doorway. Ten minutes passed as I sat and stared out the barred windows onto the dusty street outside. She reappeared with a younger man.

"Sanbainuu," I said and pointed at the menu inquisitively.

He shook his head. I pointed at a few other items and

was met by the same response.

"Is this a restaurant?" I asked rhetorically, miming a knife and fork again.

He shook his head. "No, no."

This clearly wasn't going anywhere. "Bayarla," I replied and set off to find somewhere else.

I soon found an upmarket place that was undoubtedly a restaurant. Numerous tables were laid out with cutlery on white tablecloths. I was, however, the only customer. A bell jingled when I walked in, startling two women inside.

"Sanbainuu," I said. "Heet heet?" I mimed a knife and fork.

They looked at each other with a confused expression. I pointed at a menu. Still they stood and stared at me. What was I doing wrong?

After a few more minutes of confusing miming, one realized what I was after and lead me to a table. The food was boiled lamb on rice - a Mongolian classic. I daydreamed of eating an apple or an orange. I couldn't remember the last time I'd eaten fruit or vegetables. Beijing, probably.

—

With both Noddy and myself refuelled I set off from Khovd, eager to use the last of the daylight. The road climbed quickly into foothills and other vehicles quickly thinned away as it disappeared into a web of tracks. Soon I was alone again, navigating past enormous boulders that towered over us and sent long shadows reaching out on the grass.

The land climbed further before flattening out onto a vast, dry plateau dotted with large shrubs. As the light was weakening the tracks led to a bridge over powerful, churning river. The bridge had collapsed and the water was too high and fast to cross.

The only option was to follow the river to find a suitable crossing point. Steep, imposing hills made an upstream crossing unlikely, so I turned Noddy and found some animal tracks heading downstream.

A shout cut through the sound of running water. I stopped Noddy and turned in the direction of the voice. A young girl was waving at me from a ger hidden amongst some tall bushes. I motored over and she was joined by a woman who I assumed was her mother, another teenage girl, and a young boy and girl, neither older than five or six.

I removed my helmet. "Sanbainuu," I offered with a smile.

"Sanbainuu," the girl replied with a giggle. The other children laughed.

I pointed at the river, then shrugged and patted Noddy. The girl pointed downstream an made an arch with her hands. A bridge.

"Bayarla," I said with a smile.

The mother pointed at their ger and mimed a drink. I accepted gladly and followed them inside. It was a tidy place, just a few beds ringing walls supported by a wooden lattice. The ceiling fabric was held in place by wood radiating away from the chimney. Clothes hung on lines strung up across the gers' frame. Two baby goats lay in a small pen just near the doorway.

The mother quickly procured a bowl of steaming soup. I took it with a smile, nodding and repeating "Bayarla" many times. They all giggled at me and the youngest children quickly overcame their shyness as we bypassed the language barrier with smiles and gestures. They showed me their baby goats and I showed them Noddy, sitting them on the seat and allowing them to rev the engine while the mother looked on with a grin. We took some photos together and the older girls and their mother laughed and hid their faces in their hands when I showed them the images on my camera.

The sun slowly made progress towards the horizon. I still had another hour or so of light and didn't want to impose on the family, so after a merry goodbye I struck off in the direction they indicated.

A bridge soon loomed over the river, seemingly brand new, although the road on either side remained unpaved. I set up camp on a dry stretch of riverbank and took the opportunity to remove all my clothes for a wash. The water was glacially cold but crystal clear. I lay flat in the rapids and submerged my head, letting the icy river strip the dust and sweat and heat away with cold, gentle hands.

—

The following day, the fifth since setting out from Moron, I finally climbed into the Altai. The foothills stood and became towering cliffs that hemmed us in to narrow, dark rocky valleys. We passed many vehicles heading both directions. Each valley led to another and the road climbed gradually upwards until the walls of rock began to shrink down again.

Around midday we came to the top of a small rise that led down onto a vast open plain, ringed by white hills and dotted with lakes the same blue as the sky. The clouds lay low overhead, like a herd of fluffy white sheep slowly making their way to pastures beyond the distant snowy hills.

I wound my way past a few lakes then stopped to eat and take some photos. The air was cooler and fresher with a hint of snow. I sat next to Noddy, spooning mouthfuls of hot noodles and enjoying the view. I wondered whether anyone had walked to those distant hilltops, whether the snow bore footprints at all. Maybe I should walk up one. Or maybe not. It's probably far higher than it looks.

I stood and returned to Noddy. When I pressed the ignition, however, he could only manage a few weak coughs. I tried again with the same result. I tried a third time, opening the throttle to give him a bit more juice. He spluttered to life.

We rode on. The land remained open, showing views of lakes bordered by bare hills with a backdrop of snow-capped peaks against a bright blue sky. I could see eagles wheeling far above, scouring the green and brown grasslands rolling away below. The steppe no longer seemed as threatening as it had the day before and appeared to be offering a last, spectacular view.

The sun travelled fast across the sky and the hours dropped away. Noddy cruised along with his high-pitched drone, as eager as I was to rest. In the mid-afternoon the road bent around a steep hillside to reveal Bayan Olgii, a town of colourful roofs nestled between jagged hills.

We'd made it. The first night I'd spent on the steppe was a distant memory. I was dirty, physically exhausted, mentally drained and covered in insect bites. After all those kilometres of grass and sand, the mechanics and hill starts, over rocks and plains and deserts and mountains, we were both here, in the far west of Mongolia. At long last, I thought, I can finally poo behind a closed door.

12
THE VALLEYS

I was once again faced with the decision of how to continue. The central question was whether or not to sell Noddy as I'd originally planned. Time was pressing. My visa was running out and I needed to get to the Russian border with a few days to spare in case the crossing was closed. The time pressure meant that I could only sell Noddy at a significant loss. Anyone looking to buy him could simply wait me out. Keeping Noddy would be cheaper, but I wasn't sure if he'd be allowed into Russia. Even if he was, I'd then have to ride across half of the entire Eurasian continent at sixty kilometres per hour.

In the end, leaving Noddy just wasn't right. For all his faults he'd carried me, somewhat faithfully, across Mongolia. Selling him in Olgii would be a premature end to our relationship. I also just couldn't really be bothered, if I'm honest. It was probably going to be a lot of hassle.

I spent a day in a mechanic's workshop. Noddy needed new tires and an oil change, although the mechanic also replaced the broken speedometer and odometer. He was ethnically Kazakh and had green eyes. In fact, many people I passed on the street had piercing green or blue eyes - something I wasn't used to after several months in Asia. Even the town itself was distinct, with blue-tipped minarets rising above the dusty streets and walled compounds. It was as if I'd already left Mongolia behind on the other side of those dark mountain passes.

I set off early the next morning. I was eager to get to Russia. The call of home was growing stronger with each passing day. No more breakdowns, no more rocks, no more sand. From here it was smooth paved roads all the way to

Switzerland. Noddy was still having difficulty starting his engine, but at least he could start. That was not today's problem.

The unpaved road climbed higher out of Olgii. The air was cold, the coldest it had yet been. I was wearing a leather jacket, a raincoat underneath, a thick woollen jumper underneath that and a shirt underneath that, and still it was like standing naked in an Arctic wind. We soon hit the cloud line and rode through a mist so thick that cold water began seeping down my neck and into my clothes. I started shivering uncontrollably and considered making a coffee to warm up, but it started to rain.

I pressed on, resolving to stop at the next village. The rain came down harder and steadily wormed its way through my boots until my socks were damp. I began to lose sensation in my feet. The icy wind passed effortlessly through my layers of clothing, stripping any remaining heat from my skin. The shivering spread from my chest to my shoulders and down to my thighs, and my teeth hammered against each other furiously. Riding a motorcycle is an extremely windy experience and at no time did I wish for the comfort of a car more than in that moment. I was shaking so badly that it was becoming hard to ride. I had to pull over.

The road descended out of the clouds into a flat plateau. I could see a village lying to the right of the road and opened the throttle with relief. The wind strengthened instantly, but all I cared about was a hot tea in some sheltered spot.

As I turned right off the main road and rode towards the village, I passed a man standing outside a walled compound. He waved and beckoned. I waved back when I rode past, then braked on an impulse. Maybe he knew somewhere where I could get a tea and some hot food.

"Sanbainuu!" he said as I removed my helmet. "Hello!"

"Sanbainuu," I replied. "Drink?" I made a drinking

motion and pointed towards town.

"Here, here," he replied. He was a thin guy with dark eyes. "Tea here."

"Here?"

He pointed to a gate in the wall behind him and beckoned me to move the bike into his yard. I thought back to the family in the ger by the river. They were friendly enough. I'm sure this guy is too.

I followed him inside and leaned Noddy onto his kickstand. The man closed the gates behind me.

"Hello!" he repeated and extended a hand. "English?"

"Yes, English." I shook his hand. "I'm Ewen. What is your name?"

"My name, Monkhbat. Good good. Cold! You must be cold on this bike. Where do you go? Rossiya?"

"Yeah, to the border. Is it much further?" I pulled my gloves off and stuffed them in my jacket pockets.

"No, no, not far, not far. But today is Saturday, border closed, no?"

"I'm not sure," I replied. "Some people say it is open, some say it is closed."

He shrugged. "Maybe closed, but you see. First, tea. Come."

He opened the door into his house and ushered me inside. It was a spacious place, slightly dim in the early morning. A large wooden table sat in a kitchen that opened into a larger room with a couch bed in the middle. Three young children lay sleeping, two boys and a girl. They stirred slightly as Monkhbat closed the door behind us.

A woman came around the corner holding a small baby and stopped when she saw me. Monkhbat spoke to her in Mongolian before introducing us.

"This my wife, this my wife. Tsetseg."

She smiled shyly, then moved into the kitchen. Monkhbat pulled out a chair for me.

"Sit, sit! You need tea."

"Tea would be great," I admitted. "Thanks so much! It's freezing out there."

Monkhbat nodded. "Yes, cold in mountains. Tsetseg make bread, you come good time."

"I don't mean to intrude," I said. "Tea is ok, honestly, thanks!"

He shook his head. "No, is ok, bread already made! Hot!"

Tsetseg soon set a steaming loaf on the table and went back to the other room while Monkhbat and I chatted amiably. His English was good. He was in the military, he told me, and had been posted here with his family. I told him of my trip and of my plans in Russia.

The children woke to the sound of our conversation and were soon curiously playing with my helmet. I spent about an hour in his warm kitchen, entertaining the kids, eating freshly made bread and drinking litres of hot tea until the warmth made it to my bones.

The conversation eventually came to a natural pause. The border called. I rose to leave and Monkhbat stood with me.

"Thanks so much, Monkhbat," I said, shaking his hand. "Please thank Tsetseg for me, the bread was excellent. Thank you."

"No problem, no problem. If border closed, come back, you can stay, no problem. I wish you good luck in Rossiya."

"Ok, I will. Thank you again, you've really made my morning!"

We walked out to the courtyard. I put my helmet and

gloves on, waved goodbye and set off for the border. The road was still unpaved and corrugated, but I didn't mind.

The road passed through the last hills and opened into a magnificent green steppe. I could see a small cluster of buildings, which turned out to be a tiny village built around the border post. I pulled into the village and arrived at the edge of Mongolia.

Several trucks were parked in front of a yellow boom gate. This wasn't a good sign.

I pulled up alongside and Noddy turned himself off. I looked down, confused, and tried to start him again. He coughed pathetically. I tried again, opening the throttle as far as I could and he coughed again before igniting. I held the throttle open in neutral, keeping the engine revving, then let go. He turned himself off again. I decided to ignore his tantrum and walked over to the yellow gate. A soldier strode across the road.

"Sanbainuu," I called out. He turned to me. "Russki? Rossiya?"

He shook his head, then pointed at his watch. "No."

"When?" I asked, dismayed.

He strode towards me abruptly and drew some squares in the dust on the side of a truck.

"Today, no." He crossed out the first square. "This, no." He crossed out the second square and pointed at the third. "This, yes."

I groaned inwardly, faced with another decision. I had three options. I could either ride back to Olgii through the rain and the cold and spend a day there, ride back to Monkhbat's, or set up camp here. The last option seemed easiest.

The soldier sensed my thought process and pointed to a building on the other side of the road, behind a wooden fence. He made a pillow with his hands. I thanked him and walked over to investigate. It was a small guesthouse. An older lady swiftly ushered me in when I walked through her gates. She charged a lot for a bed, so I pointed at the grass outside and made a sleeping motion. She looked doubtful at the idea but agreed to let me camp there for a cheaper rate.

Relieved, I began unpacking. It was the late morning and although I was initially dismayed at the thought of spending a weekend in this tiny village I was now beginning to look forward to it. There was nowhere to go, no place to be, so I could just read my book and go for walks in the hills, unconnected and uncaring.

Except my iPad was missing. I swore softly, then rechecked my pack. It wasn't there. I began pulling my things out urgently and swore louder. It was gone. It wasn't in my bag of valuables, it wasn't in my pack, it wasn't even wrapped up mistakenly in my sleeping bag. It was gone. My books, my photos, all on there. Gone.

I took some deep breaths and retraced my steps. I was sure I'd packed everything when I left Olgii. I had also double checked the ger and there had been nothing there. No, I can't have left it in Olgii. Maybe... maybe Monkhbat took it? Something surged in my gut. Surely not.

I found the woman again and asked her through a series of urgent hand gestures if she could keep an eye on my pack. She agreed. I shouldered my small backpack of important items, emptied half the emergency jerry can into Noddy's tank and revved him to life. He growled and leaped off when I opened the throttle, unburdened by my baggage.

We flew back across the steppe at the fastest speed Noddy had ever mustered. The road was too corrugated to handle at this pace so I kept to the narrow but smoother side tracks, weaving around the rocks that littered the ground with now-practiced hands. Noddy responded to each twist of the throttle with a roar and a burst of fresh energy. It was as if he knew my urgency. There was nobody in the world that could catch us here, on this terrain we knew so well, we man and machine.

The village soon appeared. I could see a car pulling out of Monkhbat's house and driving towards the highway with its left indicator blinking. He was heading towards Olgii. I had to cut him off at the intersection. I twisted the throttle and Noddy surged forward eagerly, his engine straining as it reached capacity.

I reached the intersection first and slowed down before turning towards the car, then parked Noddy in the middle of the road. The car came to a quick stop when I waved a hand. I smiled, removed my helmet and waved again. I still wasn't sure that Monkhbat had my iPad, so I intended to stay friendly.

Monkhbat opened the driver's door and stepped out. He held his hands up and looking at me with wide, panicked eyes. Tsetseg sat in the passenger seat, clutching a child. Her face was white and wide-eyed in an expression of raw terror. I'd never seen anyone look at me that way. The realization sunk in.

I took a deep breath.

"Problem? No problem?" Monkhbat rushed his words.

"I'm just looking for an iPad," I made a square with my hands and pointed at his house.

"Ok, we talk inside, we talk inside, ok?" He kept his hands in the air.

"Sure," I replied. He did a quick U-turn and I followed him into his compound. Tsetseg and the children got out as soon as the car stopped. The kids looked at me with wide eyes before Tsetseg quickly ushered them away, leaving Monkhbat and I alone in the courtyard. He held his hands up again as if I was holding him at gunpoint.

"What is problem? What is problem?" he asked, eyeing me. I glanced around, suddenly wary.

"I'm looking for my iPad," I said.

"I don't know, I don't know," he pleaded. "What do you want?"

"Let's go inside," I said, moving towards him. All I wanted was to get my iPad and leave.

He turned and lead me into the kitchen, then turned to face me. I pulled out my phone.

"It's like this, but bigger." I drew a square in the air.

"My child, he took it," Monkhbat said, standing on the other side of the table. The air was thick with tension. His voice rose with every sentence. Tsetseg and the kids were nowhere to be seen.

"We get in car to look for him."

"Your son took it? Where is he?"

"I don't know, he take, we get in car to find you. We come tell you."

I shook my head. "Were you going to look for your son, or were you coming to tell me?"

"No, I don't understand."

"You do understand, Monkhbat. Your story has changed. Were you looking for me, or for your son? Which is it?"

"I don't know, my son, look for you. We come, tell you."

"Monkhbat, if you have my iPad, just give it back and I'll get out of here. No worries."

"No, I don't know. Maybe my son take?"

"Monkhbat, please. Where is it?"

He shook his head, shrugged.

My patience ran out.

"WHERE IS IT?" I roared and took a step forward to slam a fist hard on the table. It shook under the impact and the sound exploded outwards, taking me by surprise as much as Monkhbat. He seemed to shrink slightly as he gave in.

"Ok, ok," he said. He walked into the other room, opened a cupboard and lifted up a pile of folded shirts to reveal my iPad. I let go of a deep breath. He handed it over wordlessly.

"Thank you," I said sarcastically and returned to Noddy. The jerry can had fallen off in the rush.

I found it lying on the ground on the way back to the border, cracked and broken. I won't need it in Russia, I thought. There'd be paved roads and petrol stations all the way home.

—

I returned to the guesthouse to find a young couple sitting at the kitchen table, who I assumed to be Russian. He was a tall guy with a full head of curly hair and she was small and heavily pregnant, with kind, shy eyes.

They looked up at the sound of my boots clunking into the room. "Uh, hi," I offered. "Russki?"

"Da," the man replied. "Ty? Russki?"

"Uh, nyet," I said. "Angli? English?"

"Ah, English, ok," he said with a smile. "I know... some English. Not good."

"It's probably better than my Russian," I laughed. "I'm Ewen."

"Ewen," he repeated, shaking my hand. "My name is Sasha. This Elena, my wife. Her English, uh, not good."

Elena smiled at me and stayed silent.

"What part of Russia are you from?" I asked, pulling out a chair.

"Novosibirsk," Sasha said. "Both from Novosibirsk."

"And what are you guys doing in Mongolia?"

Sasha leaned forward. "Sorry, what? Uh… repeat please."

"Why are you in Mongolia?"

"Ah, in Mongolia. We are, uh, scientist." His accent was heavy. "Study, uh… how you say in English? Leopard?"

"Leopards?" I asked. "In Mongolia?"

"Da, yes. Snow leopards. We collect the cameras in the mountains."

"You're kidding. I thought there were no snow leopards left! You have videos?"

"Da, many. I show you, if you want."

Sasha pulled a laptop out of his bag and opened a folder full of videos. They'd captured footage of furry snow leopards walking past the cameras, sniffing carefully and marking rocks against the backdrop of the Altai, high lakes and white hills.

We spoke for a while about their work while we watched, although Sasha did most of the talking. Elena remained quiet, nodding and smiling on occasion. Sasha was writing his PhD and they both worked for a Russian conservation group documenting snow leopard numbers in Mongolia and southern Siberia. Sasha spent most of the summer in the mountains, retrieving camera traps and setting new ones. Elena was taking time off to have their second baby. The first, Yaroslav, was in Novosibirsk with Sasha's mum.

"And what you do in Russia?" Sasha asked when he folded the laptop away.

"I'm not sure yet," I said. "I would love to see a lot, but it is a big country. I will go to Novosibirsk first, then I must figure out how to get to Moscow."

"And why you here? You have bike?"

"Yes, that one there." I pointed out the window. "I

bought it in Ulaanbaatar and rode it here."

"You rode to here, from Ulaanbaatar?" Sasha asked incredulously. "And now you ride to Russia?"

"If they let me in," I chuckled.

Sasha raised his eyebrows. "I think maybe you are crazy. But if you want, I can help you to cross border."

"Could you?" I asked. "If it's not too much trouble, that would be a great help."

He shrugged. "Of course, it is no problem. And in Russia, where you go?"

"Novosibirsk first," I said. "Then to Moscow and then probably Latvia."

"That is, uh, a very long drive."

"It is, and the bike goes very slowly."

The conversation paused. Elena spoke to Sasha in Russian and looked at me. He nodded.

"Elena wants to know, if you like, we go for walk?"

"Absolutely," I said. "A walk sounds grand."

We put jackets on and struck off. Sasha lead us along a thinning path up a hill that loomed over the village. On foot the landscape suddenly seemed much, much larger. The shadows of clouds passed across the treeless expanse, hurried along by a persistent wind. A row of mountains peeked over the distant rolling hills. Those, Sasha told me, were in Russia. We stood at the top of the hill, surveying all the open land before us and squinting in the wind.

"You know how high we are?" Sasha asked.

"No idea."

"Two thousand five hundred metre."

"Two thousand five hundred? It doesn't look that high."

He nodded. "Is flat, yes, but very high. The mountains there, three thousand five hundred metre."

I looked over at the distant peaks. They were just visible over the edge of the steppe, their tops hidden in clouds that did, now that I looked up, seem low. The altitude, I suddenly realized, explained why Noddy had been turning himself off. The air was so thin that the engine couldn't muster enough power to idle.

—

The three of us spent most of the weekend together. The guesthouse filled with rowdy Russian truck drivers and the entire town, including the drivers and the woman running the guesthouse, drank vodka from the early morning. Most were drunk by midday. They shouted at each other and stumbled through the streets. We escaped by going on more walks up windy hills on the vast, open steppe. The village may have been a depressing place, but my last views of Mongolia were no less breathtaking than the first.

We rose early on Monday as the trucks began rumbling, ready to cross into Russia. A soldier waved me forward ahead of Sasha and Elena.

I spent some time in Mongolian customs while they inspected Noddy's paperwork. I was nervous, worried that I couldn't take him with me, but after an hour or so I was cleared to leave.

I walked back out to Noddy, swung a leg over and hopped into place. I looked behind when I rode off. The steppe stared back, confidently meeting my gaze until I turned back around and left it there, waiting.

The road wound through steepening hills for a few kilometres until it passed through a tall chain-link fence stretching as far as I could see. A large sign in Cyrillic and English made clear what this was: "You are now entering the territory of the Russian Federation."

A small brick building and a watchtower guarded the road. A soldier with an automatic rifle slung over his back waved me over. He inspected my paperwork and Noddy, spoke to someone through a radio, then waved me on.

The Russian border post itself was a few kilometres further along the road. A long queue had already formed and after a few hours of waiting I began the tedious process of standing at different desks and answering questions. Sasha found me and helped me navigate the complexities. It took time but I was eventually cleared. We shook hands and I agreed to call him when I reached Novosibirsk.

I walked outside to find a group of armed policemen and a sniffer dog standing around Noddy. One beckoned to me.

"Angliiski?"

"Yes, English," I said.

"This is your bike?" he pointed at Noddy. The dog sniffed ominously at my pack.

"Yeah, that's mine. Do you want to have a look?"

"Oh no, no problem. I just want to say, nice bike!" He gave me a thumbs-up. "Have a good time in Russia!"

"Oh, ok! Thanks!" I said with relief.

I got back on Noddy and pulled forward slowly, scanning around in case another guard waved me over. Just as I was about to clear the last gate a soldier walked out of a small building and held a hand up to stop me. I switched Noddy's engine off. I'd left Mongolia at ten in the morning and it was now two in the afternoon. How much longer would I be here?

The soldier stood in front of Noddy and indicated that I should remove my helmet.

"English?"

"Yes, English."

"Why are you entering Russia?"

I looked at him, unsure what a good answer would be.

"Uh, because I want to see it? For tourism?"

"But why?" he asked sternly, his thumbs hooked on his belt.

"Well, it is a big country with lots to see."

"And you visit Russia on this motorcycle?" He looked dubiously at Noddy.

I patted the fuel tank. "Yep, on this!"

He shook his head. "This I think is crazy, but you come to a beautiful country. I hope you have a very good time." He extended a hand. "Welcome to Russia!"

—

He was right about it being a beautiful country. I rode along a smooth road and entered a steep land of green mountain valleys filled with long grass and grazing horses, all flanked by crowds of pine trees climbing up to distant mountaintops. It was the first time I'd seen trees in a while. They seemed like strange, motionless creatures, crowded along a brown river that rushed torrents of water through this narrow green corridor.

The road wound its way on the edge of these valleys and bent around sheer cliffs that rose suddenly out of the lush alpine landscape. Ramshackle wooden farmsteads were the only buildings in sight. And there were butterflies, so many butterflies, fluttering above the green earth or hanging in suspended animation amongst beams of sunlight above the thick grass and meadow flowers. It was as if I'd left Mongolia and entered a storybook set in the ancient Swiss Alps. Even the sound of birds chirping was a novelty after the silence of the Mongol steppe. The road was paved, there were road signs, bus stops, speed limits, long grass, pedestrian crossings, big trees – in a heartbeat I'd gone from Asia to Europe. Home surely wasn't far away.

Overland

I quickly snapped back to reality when a butterfly smacked straight into my larynx and left me gasping in my helmet. Another then slammed into the plastic visor with a percussive crack. It's amazing that a small, harmless creature can pack such a punch when it hits your throat at seventy kilometres an hour.

I camped next to the road that night and kept anything containing food outside my tent in case of bears. In the end, the only threat to my well-being came from the swarm of enormous mosquitoes that descended as soon as dusk fell across the valley. I lay in my sleeping bag and enjoyed a Mars bar while the swarm whined outside the tent. The air was calm. I was finally in Russia, with only one border crossing left between here and home.

—

I woke to a drizzly morning. Dew covered the long grass and quickly soaked through my boots and socks while I rolled up the wet tent and packed Noddy, then set off in what was now a familiar routine.

After a few hours the mountain valleys lowered into rolling forested foothills, which in turn eventually gave way to a flat plain of silver birch groves and green farmlands. I was making great progress, especially compared to the speeds I was doing in Mongolia. Noddy was averaging at least sixty kilometres an hour. I pulled over and checked my phone to see how close I was to Novosibirsk.

The little blue arrow had hardly moved from the border. Confused, I put the phone away and pressed on, when shortly I came to a sign – Novosibirsk, 890 kilometres.

890? I looked at my phone again. How could it be 890 kilometres from here? At Noddy's speed, this was fifteen hours of riding at least.

My morale crashed. Almost a thousand kilometres of flat farmlands lay ahead and that was just to the nearest city. I knew Russia was big, but that was just insane.

To add to the tediousness of the journey, Noddy's increased speeds meant the wind completely drowned out the small headphones I'd been using to listen to music now and again. I was totally alone to dwell on how far I had yet to go. All of a sudden Noddy had become a massive burden.

The hours dragged by unwillingly. Then, when I was riding up a hill, Noddy suddenly started skidding all over the road. My heart launched into my throat and I only just managed to keep him upright before pulling over.

The rear tyre had blown. I'd already used all my spares. Brilliant. Not only was I nowhere, I was stuck in nowhere. I rubbed my face with my hands.

The only real option I had was to ask for help. I stuck my hand out and the first car pulled over, followed immediately by the next. There was a middle-aged man in the first and an old couple in the second. They looked at my tyre and tutted. After working out that I couldn't speak Russian and they couldn't speak English, the woman revealed that she spoke some German.

"Don't worry, we call the emergency service," she said. "Where are you going?"

"Novosibirsk," I said. "I came from Mongolia yesterday."

She raised an eyebrow and looked at Noddy. "On that?"

I told her the whole story. She raised both eyebrows. "What do your parents think?"

"They think I'm crazy."

She laughed. "I think they're right!"

Not long after her husband made a phone call, a tow

truck appeared and soon we were on our way in convoy. I was in the car with the younger man, who was the son of the older couple. Shortly we came to a mechanic and unloaded Noddy. The woman and her husband spoke with the mechanic in Russian.

She turned to me. "This is Sergei. He will take care of you. Do you have enough money for a new tyre?"

"Yes," I said. "Thank you. And how much should I pay the tow truck?"

She waved her hand. "Don't worry, we have paid them. Now here's my husband's number – make sure you call us when you arrive in Novosibirsk! I am worried for you! Drive safe."

Sergei was a rough-looking guy with short cropped hair, a lean look and a cigarette hanging loosely out of his mouth. He looked me in the eyes and shook my hand with a grin.

He quickly set to work taking Noddy's wheel off, removed the faulty tyre and tried patching the inner tube. After an hour of failed attempts he drove me into Gorno-Altaysk, the nearest town, and helped me find a new tyre. The butterflies were still floating everywhere amidst dazzling green foliage. I stared out the window in amazement at the trees, the river, the apartment buildings that seemed so enormous, the colourful billboards and bridges and cars. There was so much green here, so much water!

After another hour Sergei had Noddy up and running with new tyres and patched-up inner tubes. It had taken most of his morning.

I asked him how much I owed him as we stood outside his workshop. He shook his head and waved the money away, puffing on a cigarette. I pressed him but he flatly refused, shook my hand and waved me off. I thanked him profusely. Again, it was all I could do.

So, by the kindness of strangers, I eventually made it to Novosibirsk and parked next to a large square in the city centre. A clear blue sky had brought everyone out and about. Children were cycling around on small bikes and peering curiously into the pools of large fountains under the watchful gaze of attentive parents. There were so many people everywhere, so much traffic.

I borrowed a stranger's phone and called Sasha, who soon came and met me in his car with Elena and their two-year-old son, Yaroslav. It was a relief to see them. We went for dinner in a nearby café.

"How was the ride?" Sasha asked with a knowing smile.

"Beautiful at first," I replied. "But very long!"

"You know, it is three thousand kilometres to Moscow and road is flat, very flat. Are you planning on riding? It take you five days and probably many problems."

"I don't know," I said. "I think I will take the train. Do you know where to go?"

"You could take train, yes, but I am also going to Moscow in a truck."

"You are? What for?"

Yaroslav giggled in his pram, prompting Elena to shush him.

"I have an interview, with, uh, WWF? You know?"

"The World Wildlife Fund?"

"Sorry, uh… repeat, please?"

I spoke slower. "The World Wildlife Fund?"

"Ah, yes, Wildlife Fund. Also I take some things to my brother, in Samara. If you like, you can, uh, stay in our flat with Elena and me, then in three days we go to my brother and then to Moscow."

"Sasha, I'll say yes, but you know you don't have to. You can say no. Honestly."

He waved me off. "Is no problem. You stay with us and we can show you some of Siberia."

"And this is ok with Elena?"

Sasha spoke to her in Russian. She nodded at me and smiled.

"She says yes, of course, it is no problem!"

We hid Noddy at a cottage belonging to Sasha's mum and drove to Sasha and Elena's apartment, which was on the fifteenth floor of a typical Soviet-style apartment building far outside the city. A small, rickety elevator took us up to their small flat; one bathroom, a kitchen and a living room. Sasha and Elena slept on a fold-out couch bed in the living room next to Yaroslav in a small cot. I slept on a cushioned bench next to the kitchen table. The view looked out to four other identical apartment blocks and over wooden cottages with colourful roofs partially hidden in a green birch forest. The land was entirely flat, stretching away until the Earth curved below the sky.

—

Sasha and Elena did not have much. They were students starting a family - not the ideal circumstance to host a backpacker they'd only met two days ago. It was difficult to impose on them, but equally difficult to pass up the offer. It was as if I'd always lived there, just an old friend who had recently returned home.

A lot of the food they ate was grown in the garden of Sasha's mum's cottage (dacha, in Russian) - strawberries, lettuce, carrots, potatoes and jam made from honeyberries, which are a sort of long thin blueberry native to Siberia.

We spent a day there working in the garden. Elena and I collected bowls full of honeyberries, mashed them and we all ate the jam out of mugs while we sat around a low table in the dacha. It was a cosy place with a low wooden ceiling. The bursting garden was just visible through small windows. Yaroslav squealed when Elena spoon-fed him mashed berries. Sasha and his mum tried to teach me Russian and laughed at my botched efforts. I laughed with them, happy to spend a sunny day picking berries and drinking tea here in this quiet corner of the world.

Over the next few days Sasha and Elena showed me around the region. We went to Akademgorodok, an old Soviet science centre that is now one of Russia's top universities. It used to be an intellectual haven in Soviet times, Sasha told me, as we walked along shortcuts through the surrounding birch forest. Residents were allowed to watch musical performances and listen to poetry. It is still an exclusive area that is home to some of Novosibirsk's richest people, who live in large houses on leafy streets that wouldn't be out of place in suburban America. He also mentioned that they regularly see bears on campus.

Later that same afternoon we went to a beach on the shores of a huge lake outside the city. Sasha told me that the lake was created in Soviet times, so the bottom was covered in dead trees. We kept talking, about their work, about Danika, about Novosibirsk, about Russia. Yaroslav was fascinated by the waves lapping gently against the sand. Elena tried to take him into the water, but he cried and squirmed away.

On another day Sasha offered to take me to a local swimming hole. I was under the impression this was nearby – in fact, that is the exact word Sasha used – but it turned out to be two hundred kilometres away. 'Nearby' is a relative concept in Siberia. We loaded up the car in the morning and set off with Yaroslav cooing happily in the back seat.

Overland

After an hour on the motorway, we turned off the road and followed a sand track through a dark forest. The trees crowded us in on either side, pushed back only occasionally by villages dotted with rusting Soviet-era tractors. Yaroslav and Elena soon fell asleep. I stared out the window and deep into the trees.

The Russian countryside was a world apart. Novosibirsk was a European city with opera houses, fashion chains, Starbucks and McDonalds, but out here nothing had changed in decades. Men still loaded logs onto carts pulled by donkeys and drove them along unpaved roads through these villages fashioned from the endless, endless forest.

We eventually arrived at the swimming hole. It was a disused quarry that was now a lake filled with large fish. A small group of trees perched on a small rocky island in the middle. There were a few other people around, sunning themselves on the lakeside or pushing paddleboats in large circles around the island. Sasha and I spent the time trying to teach Yaroslav how to swim. He squealed in the cold water and clung to Sasha's arms. Elena laughed from the lakeside.

I entertained a daydream of what my life would look like if I decided to never leave. Probably cold, I reckoned, and filled with mashed honeyberry jam.

13
THE MEADOWS

Eventually the time came to go, however much I wished it wouldn't. We woke at three in the morning. I hugged Elena, thanking her as much as I could, then shouldered my pack again and waited in the hallway while Sasha kissed her and a bleary-eyed Yaroslav goodbye.

We drove back to the dacha to fetch Noddy, strapped him onto the back of the truck amongst all the stuff destined for Sasha's brother and set off in the pre-dawn light. Novosibirsk was just visible as a cluster of low buildings when we crossed the mighty Ob river, heading west.

For most of the first day we drove across an enormous swamp just north of the border with Kazakhstan. The land was totally flat, nothing but silver birch trees and marsh. It is the largest swamp in the world, Sasha told me - larger than Western Europe. There were villages in there that are only accessible in winter, when the water freezes over. Russia is so impossibly large. You could live in that swamp your whole life and never know a hill or a dry patch of grass.

The road signs ticked down the kilometres to the next city – Omsk, 700 kilometres, Chelyabinsk, 1500 kilometres, Moscow, 3500 kilometres. I thought I was used to vast distances; Russia was on another level. Novosibirsk to Moscow was a long way, but that wasn't even close to halfway across the country. Vladivostok, on the Pacific, was well over five thousand kilometres in the other direction. I looked north out the window at the birch trees sliding endlessly by. There was nothing that way but almost two thousand kilometres of swamp, taiga forest and vast, ice-covered tundra.

The hours ticked by. We drifted in and out of conversation and in and out of petrol stations. The truck guzzled gas. We were splitting costs but I was rapidly using the last of my money.

Omsk came and went. We listened to an Altaian throat singing band on repeat while the sun rose, hung overhead, then lowered. I slept, looked out the window, then slept some more. Sasha stared resolutely out the windscreen. He showed no signs of getting tired.

Chelyabinsk came and went. I saw my first European Union license plate on a Lithuanian truck just outside the city, which was a short moment of excitement before I drifted back into a daze.

As the sun was going down the land finally started rising slowly. The swamp stopped and the birch trees gradually gave way to a mix of green leaves and pine, interspersed with meadows with butterflies floating over purple and yellow flowers. The sun was hitting the landscape sideways, throwing long shadows and giving everything that golden hue at the end of a summer day. We saw smoke rising from the road ahead and soon passed a truck with its brakes on fire. The forest flickered in the light.

We were, I realized, in the Ural Mountains. And so, on some remote hilltop in southern Russia, somewhere north of the Caspian Sea, I left Asia behind and crossed into Europe.

We didn't stop until sometime past midnight (although I wasn't sure what time zone we were in) and slept in our seats.

After what was essentially an extended power nap, Sasha started the truck and we set off again. A sign gave the distance to Samara – 450 kilometres.

The land flattened in the dawn light and became vast fields of yellow and green, a far more human landscape than the one we'd left on the other side of the Urals. The fields became towns and then fields again and morning became midday before we finally pulled into Samara. Sasha rubbed his eyes while we navigated the potholed streets lined with ramshackle wooden houses, searching for his brother's new place. We eventually found it, came to a welcome stop and stretched our forgotten legs.

Sasha's brother came from the house and introduced himself as Alexei. He was shirtless and wore a gold necklace with a large cross.

Alexei invited us inside and fed us strawberry jam alongside his wife, father-in-law and some random man. I never discovered this guy's relationship to anybody because the conversation was entirely in Russian, with the occasional laugh in my direction.

After a while Alexei pointed to me and said something to Sasha.

"He wants to know if you know what a banya is," Sasha said.

"No idea."

"It is shower," Sasha said. "Come, I show you."

We got up and Alexei led us around the back of his house to a small wooden shack behind a vegetable garden. He grabbed some towels off a clothesline and handed them to us, then went back to join the others.

Sasha led the way into the shack. It was a small wooden room with a couch placed across from a fire that was burning hot in a wood-fired stove. Several bundles of birch branches hung on a string across the middle of the room. On the right, just past the stove, a closed door led to another room.

I eyed the branches. I'd seen something about these on Long Way Round, Ewan and Charley went to a Russian sauna.

They got naked and were belted by two other naked men with these branches. Were Sasha and I about to strip naked and whip each other? I hoped not, but I had no choice. I was too far in to back out now. If getting myself and Noddy to Moscow meant getting naked in a steamy room with a big Russian and beating the balls off each other with sticks, then so be it.

Sasha removed his clothes and motioned that I should do the same. He then went into the other room and closed the door. I sat on the couch in my undies and wondered when the whipping would begin. The room was hot and soon I was sweating.

After several minutes Sasha came out again.

"Come in," he said, beckoning. "Shower."

I followed. Inside this room, which was smaller than the other, was a big metal bin filled with water and a boiler attached to the back of the fireplace. Shelves along the wooden wall were lined with shampoo and soap.

"This is cold," said Sasha, pointing at the metal bin, "and this is hot." He indicated the boiler. "I will wait outside."

I breathed a sigh of relief.

After a wash we unloaded Alexei's belongings and set off again. We drove the rest of the day across flat farmlands. We crossed the Volga river in the afternoon. It was the limit of the Nazi advance into Russia, Sasha told me. He had lost a grandfather in the war, as had most people in Russia. That is why, he explained, there were large monuments in every village we passed through.

We then continued on for hours upon hours. I stared out the window, listened to podcasts and slept, while Sasha stared single-mindedly at the road ahead. I offered to drive on several occasions but he politely declined.

Sasha woke me from sleep in the early evening. The

light outside was fading.

"Ewen, I must ask, where do you stay?"

"Hm?" I was groggy.

"We are almost in Moscow. I stay at friend's house, outside city, but where you go?"

"Oh, right. I'm not sure, but if we see a motel or something I can just stay there."

"You are sure? I sorry, is uh... not possible to stay with me."

"No, honestly Sasha that's fine, you've put up with me long enough! A motel is ok."

One appeared on the side of the road shortly afterwards. We pulled in and ate a quick dinner of re-heated pizza from the motel's canteen.

It was an odd place, I thought, to say goodbye. I'd met Sasha in Mongolia and now I was with him here, only a hundred kilometres outside Moscow. Is he sure he isn't coming to Basel with me? How did I get here so quickly?

We unloaded Noddy and I turned him on for the first time in almost a week. He came alive.

I turned to Sasha, unsure how to say goodbye.

"Sasha, I don't know what to say. Thank you. I know it doesn't mean much, but if you're ever in Europe with a crap motorcycle and you need a lift to Moscow, let me know!"

He laughed. "Is ok Ewen. Is uh... nice to have you. Send me email when you home."

We hugged. Sasha got back in the truck and the engine roared. Gravel crunched under the tires when he pulled away. I was alone again.

I had a long, sweet shower, then fell into a deep and dreamless sleep.

—

I was confused when I woke in the motel. What was this room? How did I... oh yeah. The drive. Sasha wasn't here.

I rubbed my eyes, stretched and stumbled into the shower. Steam filled the small space while I savoured the heat and summoned energy for the road ahead.

I was hoping to get to Moscow and have a day in the city, so I packed Noddy for the first time in a week and rode off early. But Noddy had his own plans. As we were clipping along at a steady pace on the motorway the back wheel suddenly slid back and forth. I knew instantly what he'd done. The tyre was flat again. I'd been riding for less than an hour.

"Noddy, you daft, daft bastard," I swore, leaning carefully into the next exit. "Can't we go one goddamn day without something going wrong?"

I guided him to the roadside and came to a wobbly stop. A blue sky promised a clear sunny day, but the growing sunshine failed to warm me. Noddy already felt like a dead weight, but when I stood on the side of the road somewhere outside Moscow, he began to look like a ball and chain. All he seemed to do was keep me locked up in mechanics' workshops forking out wads of money. Maybe this stupid red motorcycle had outlived its usefulness.

I looked across the road. A few beaten-up old cars lay behind a barbed-wire fence in some sort of scrapyard. I could drop Noddy there. Or maybe I could just dump him in the woods behind. Would anyone notice an old, rusting bike left to be swallowed by weeds? I would be free to take comfortable trains, to sleep as I was carried home, or to read my book while sipping a hot drink, occasionally glancing out the window to see the summer countryside passing dreamily by.

Yet here I was, stuck on the fringe of Moscow with a problem to solve. The only real option, once again, was to ask for help.

I stuck my hand out and the first vehicle pulled over. I was almost overcome by a surge of affection and relief. It was as if all of Russia was looking out for me.

The small cherry-picker truck came to a stop. The driver hopped out, had a quick look, then grinned. He pointed at his truck and indicated that we should lift Noddy on it.

"Mechanic, five hundred metre."

We unloaded my pack and hoisted Noddy onto the truck with a massive effort. The man strapped him to the folded crane with the elastic straps I used for my luggage, then gave me a quick lift to the workshop. He tooted his horn when he pulled away.

The workshop was just opening but they took Noddy into the garage and indicated that I should wait in reception. I sat a while, stewing at Noddy and sipping a hot coffee. A TV played the morning news and the receptionist tapped away at a keyboard behind her desk.

Eventually the mechanic came in and beckoned me to follow. He had inflated the tyre, but it seemed that was all he could do. To get a proper fix, he told me, I should go to another mechanic several kilometres down the road.

I got back on Noddy and followed his directions. The place wasn't hard to find but this guy simply shook his head.

"Husqvarna," he said, pointing further down the road.

With a sigh, I got back on Noddy and rode further. We soon came to a large metal gate blocking the entrance to an industrial compound. A sign just behind the gate read 'Husqvarna'. It seemed an odd place to fix a motorcycle.

A security guard sat in a booth nearby and watched me while I parked Noddy and walked to his window. I explained, through basic Russian and a lot of hand gestures, why I was there and he eventually phoned someone and let me in.

I was met by a thin guy in a suit who introduced himself as Kirill.

"Your bike, no good?" Kirill asked.

"No, flat tyre," I replied. "I've had a lot of issues with it."

"Yes, I see. Unfortunately it... uh... not possible here to fix. I take you and we fix. Wait here, one moment."

He disappeared and returned shortly with a small van. We loaded Noddy in the back and drove off the way I'd come.

Kirill asked about my trip, how I was enjoying Russia, what my plans were in Moscow. I quickly forgot my frustration at Noddy and was glad to have someone to talk to.

Kirill drove for some time along increasingly suburban streets before he parked the van in front of someone's house.

"This man, he fix for you." Kirill said. "Do not worry! I come back."

He made a phone call and shortly afterwards a shirtless guy emerged from the house. Kirill spoke with him for a minute then motioned to me. We unloaded Noddy and wheeled him around the side of the house and into a garden filled with motorcycles in various states of disrepair. This seemed like the right place, I thought.

"This man, his name is Roman," Kirill said.

"Ewen," I said to Roman, extending a hand. Roman smiled and shook my hand. He was a young guy, short, with an easy smile.

"He does not know English," Kirill continued. "But no problem. I go now, but here you stay, then I come back for you."

"No worries Kirill. Thanks so much!"

Roman quickly set to work on Noddy. After he took the back wheel off, he mimed that he needed to take it somewhere to get a new part fitted. He left me to sit in his shed and fiddle with bits of disembowelled vehicles.

Just when I pulled my iPad out of my bag to read I heard a scuffling in the yard outside. An old woman came in to the shed, wearing a cloth over her head. She yelled at me in Russian.

"Angliiski," I said, smiling. "Russki nyet."

She yelled again, louder and slower, but still in Russian.

"Uh... Angliiski?" I couldn't interpret what she was trying to say.

She beckoned me and turned on her heel back to the house. I followed.

She led me into her kitchen, sat me at the table, put a mug down and filled it with jam from a bowl. She looked at me expectantly. I ate a spoonful. I say jam, but really it was just pulverised strawberries - nice, but extremely tangy. She stared at me as I continued to eat.

I finished the mug and she yelled at me in Russian again, then loaded the mug up with more.

"Spasiba," I said with a smile. Thank you.

I ate that too under her watchful gaze. Once I'd finished she offered me another. I tried to refuse – there's only so much mashed strawberry that one person can eat - but she shouted at me and filled the mug again.

I spooned it down slowly and took a moment to consider my situation. That morning I'd hoped to be sightseeing Moscow. Instead I was sitting in a kitchen in an obscure Russian suburb being force-fed almost-jam by a loud elderly woman.

Roman returned and freed me from the force feeding. He soon had Noddy's wheel fixed and then kept fixing other things. He straightened the brake handle, repaired one of the side panels and lubricated the chain. I thanked him and offered some money, but he waved me off with a drag of his cigarette, exactly like Sergei had done.

Kirill walked into the yard when Roman was tidying up.

"The bike, is ok?"

"Yeah, it's great, thanks! Roman was fantastic."

Kirill translated for Roman, who smiled and clapped me on the back. He said something in Russian and Kirill translated back for me.

"He says, it was no problem and good luck with your trip. Now, where do you go? You need some new tubes for bike, I think."

"I do," I admitted. "And some oil and chain lubricant."

Kirill nodded. "Ok. I know place, is close to Moscow centre. Bring bike outside and follow me. I show you."

"That's ok, Kirill, if you have somewhere to be you can tell me the address! Honestly."

"The address?"

"You can show me where it is and I go."

"No, no problem. Come, follow. Not far, I show you."

I quickly loaded my stuff back onto Noddy and followed Kirill's van as he led me towards Moscow. The traffic thickened while we progressed. After half an hour we crossed a bridge and arrived at a motorcycle superstore. Kirill helped me find what I was looking for, then asked for a photo together when we returned to the car park.

"My friend," he said, putting an arm around my shoulder. "Very, very nice to meet you. Good luck with trip!"

"Kirill, I can't thank you enough," I replied. "Seriously, thank you."

He shrugged. "No problem, no problem. You need help, I help. Maybe I need help, you help, you know? Is Russian way."

I found a hostel in the city centre, only twenty minutes' walk from Red Square. Thankfully they had a private parking spot for Noddy. I unpacked, swapped my heavy riding boots for flip flops and went for a stroll to use the last few hours of daylight.

I had expected some sort of Soviet city, like Ulaanbaatar or Novosibirsk but on a much grander scale. I was wrong. The centre of Moscow was beautiful. The streets around Red Square were Parisian boulevards painted in wintry blues and greens, almost like wedding cake icing. I walked along slowly in the afternoon light, enjoying the city, the bustle, the many languages drifting past and slowly processed where I found myself. I was now closer to Basel than to Novosibirsk. Only 2500 kilometres left to go before I stopped for the night and woke up with nowhere else to go. I stopped to watch two young guys playing pop music on a violin and a cello, lost in thought, then wandered a wayward route back to my hostel.

—

I spent the next day exploring the main sights of Moscow. I started inside St Basil's Cathedral in Red Square, the one with the colourful onion roof. The inside, I was surprised to find, was actually a maze of small brick rooms.

After walking through the first floor, I took some stairs to the second and found a male a Capella choir setting up for a performance. I joined a group of others to listen. The thick walls blocked noise entering from outside, so that the only sounds were the deep voices of the choir rising and falling in harmony and occasional footsteps echoing around curved walls.

I also dropped in to see Lenin's corpse, which lies in a mausoleum on Red Square just across from the cathedral. The experience was less solemn than the Mao-soleum in Beijing, but no less weird. The queue led down some dark stairs and into an equally dark room. The only light came from Lenin's glass sarcophagus. My eyes were still adjusting to the deep gloom, so Lenin's face was all that was really visible. He still had his beard, wispy tendrils of hair that seemed to float above his waxy skin. What is it with communists and preserving dead people?

We were ushered through quickly. I emerged back into the sunlight and immediately walked to the entrance to the Kremlin, that massive red fortress by the riverbank that is the home of the Russian state. The red walls themselves were bordered by an immaculate green park of fountains and clear pools underneath little marble bridges. Little kids were swimming in one of these pools, splashing and laughing. It was a summer's day in full swing. I bought a ticket to the Kremlin and walked through, enjoying the sunshine and the sense of being in a crowd.

I made straight for the Armoury, a treasury filled with jewellery and armour collected by the Russian monarchy over the course of its history; the Russian crown jewels, the thrones and carriages of the Tsars and the Faberge Eggs. The museum and the tourists inside, who were from all over the world, were so far removed from the wooden Siberian villages I'd seen the week before that it was hard to believe I was still in the same country.

It was also hard to believe, as I wandered past ornate gowns and suits of armour, that I was only metres from Vladimir Putin's office. I wondered if he was in today and if so, what he was doing while I stood nearby, gazing at Russia's treasures.

I spent a few hours touring some of Moscow's fancy subway stations then ate dinner in a busy McDonald's, listened to the conversation of two American businessmen on the table next to mine and returned to my hostel with well-worn feet.

An excited group of teenagers were sharing my room. They were athletes of some sort who were in Moscow for a tournament. I settled on a couch in the lounge to read. I was on the final book of The Lord of the Rings. It had become somewhere to come home to at the end of every day.

14
THE END

I left Moscow early in the morning. I was hoping to get to the Latvian border by sunset, but there'd probably be a tantrum from Noddy. He seemed to be behaving well enough while I rode along Moscow's busy streets, searching for the way out of the city.

One of the difficulties of riding a motorcycle is that it's hard to follow GPS directions. I couldn't check my phone without pulling over and I couldn't pull over on main roads, so I had to memorize street names and hope I'd find them. This was made even harder by the fact that Russia uses a different alphabet. I was lost and illiterate.

After many U-turns I eventually found the westbound motorway. It quickly whisked us past office blocks and suburbs and into the countryside.

The road thinned as the day aged until it became two lanes running straight through a flat landscape of thick forest, occasionally broken by petrol stations and dirt roads leading into the trees. I sat on Noddy, held the throttle open with one hand, rested the other on my lap and watched the trees slide slowly by. I actually zoned out for so long that Noddy ran out of petrol. I had to completely empty the reserve tank to reach the next station.

I stopped in the afternoon at a roadside diner for something to eat and parked Noddy next to a group of large, expensive BMW motorcycles. The only people inside were three men, maybe aged in their late 50's, in full riding leathers and armour. I collected some food from the canteen and sat nearby.

One shortly called me over.

"Nederlands?" he asked.

I shook my head. "English."

He pointed out a window to where Noddy sat, dwarfed by their three BMWs. "That is your bike?"

"Yeah, that's mine. I'm guessing those are yours? Where have you come from?"

"From the Netherlands," he replied. He had grey hair and designer stubble. "But my friend here has come from Germany."

"Ah, cool. Has it taken you long?"

"No, no, maybe a week I think." The others nodded in agreement. "And you? Where have you come from?"

"From Mongolia," I replied. "That's where I started on the bike."

"Ah, Mongolia. That is a long way. We will ride past Mongolia, to eastern Russia and then to Japan."

"To Japan?" I asked, incredulous. "How long will that take?"

The man shrugged and translated for his friends in Dutch. Another answered. "Three weeks, maybe? But maybe faster."

"How fast do your bikes go?"

"Maybe we average one hundred kilometres each hour, sometimes more. But yours, I think, is not so fast?"

I chuckled. "No, no. It'll do sixty kilometres an hour on most days, eighty if it's in a very good mood."

"And you shipped this bike to Mongolia?"

"No, I bought it there. It was the best I could find."

The man looked at me for a second. "You bought this in Mongolia? And you ride to?"

"Switzerland."

"To Switzerland? On a bike that you buy in Mongolia?"

He translated for his friends and they grinned at me. "They say this is crazy and very slow."

I smiled. "I got a lift from Novosibirsk to Moscow. But yes, very, very slow. I wish I had a bike your size, I could be home in a few days!"

"Yes, these bikes are fast. But you do not have so far to go. Five days, maybe."

There's an instant friendship between motorcyclists. I'd found it in the nods or raised fingers I'd seen from almost every biker travelling in the opposite direction. It was like I'd joined some kind of club.

I enjoyed the conversation for a time before eventually standing to leave.

The stubbled guy stood and shook my hand. "Look, I want to ask – I work for a motorcycle magazine, sometimes I write some articles. Is it ok, for the next article, if I include some photos of you and your motorcycle?"

"Sure," I shrugged. "Do you want to take some photos now?"

We walked outside and he took some shots of Noddy, of me next to Noddy, and of all of us next to our bikes. We then mounted up and pulled off. They honked goodbye as they turned left and roared away. Noddy managed to emit a shrill whine when I turned right towards Latvia.

As the sun was starting to throw longer shadows the road wound through a postcard landscape of low, rolling hills covered in long green grass and fields of purple lavender. Insects floating lazily above the flowers, sleepy in the fading sunlight. The open country was a welcome relief from the forest. Suddenly Noddy's slow speeds weren't so bad after all. I leaned gently left, gently right, following the weaves and curves of the road. And so Russia ended much as it began – with surprisingly beautiful meadows that emerged, in unexpected greeting, while we sailed towards a tiring sun.

I arrived at the border crossing just north of Belarus at around six in the evening and left Russia without any problems. I assumed I had now crossed the most difficult borders of the trip and was relieved to join the queue to enter Latvia. This would be a quick crossing. The EU flag was flying invitingly above the border post. Fifty more metres and I was just about done with this ritual.

When my turn came I parked next to the border guard and pulled out my paperwork. By this point I'd amassed a fair amount - Noddy's vehicle passport, Mongolian insurance, transit license, etc., with all these documents translated into Russian and English. I'd lost track of what was what so I handed the whole lot over in the hope that the wall of paperwork would overwhelm the bureaucracy into submission.

"Where is this license plate from?" he asked, flicking through the papers.

"Mongolia," I replied. "I bought the bike there."

He looked at me, puzzled, then walked around the bike.

"It's a transit license," I explained, seeing the look of confusion on his face. "It's the only one they'd give me in Mongolia."

"Wait here."

He walked off to a nearby building with my passport and a few other documents. I waited under the curious gaze of other motorists waiting their turn.

The guard returned shortly afterwards, without my passport, and told me to go inside and buy European insurance. I did so and presented these new documents to the lady at the customs window.

"What is this?" she asked.

"I was told to buy this insurance and come here," I replied. She looked at me with another confused expression.

"Wait here."

She walked off with my insurance form and Noddy's vehicle passport. I waited, again, under increasingly curious stares.

She returned without my paperwork and told me to follow her. We then walked around, talked to many different border guards and were met by blank faces.

After two hours of waiting, talking, waiting and more talking, a man emerged from behind the customs window. He seemed to be some sort of manager.

"You have a bike?" he asked. "Where is it?"

I pointed to where Noddy was parked. He indicated that I should follow him and lead me over to the bike.

"You understand, there are big risks for us, letting you in," he said.

"What do you mean?"

"Well, Mongolia is a very far away country and we have not seen these papers before," he replied.

"Doesn't matter how far away it is, it's still a country and the papers are legitimate." I was tired, annoyed and unsure what he was getting at.

"It's a big risk," he repeated. "How do we solve this?"

"I don't know. You're the border guard, you tell me."

He looked at the papers. "Thirty euros?"

"What?"

"Thirty euros."

I was dumbstruck. "Are you asking me for a bribe?"

"It is not so much," he said. "Mongolia is a distant place and if not you must wait here four days to arrange a European transit number."

"Well, I don't have euros," I said and reached in my pocket to pull out the last of my Russian roubles.

"Not here!" He whispered urgently and glanced around. He then beckoned for me to follow. We walked back to the building and through a door that read "Staff Only." Suddenly the stupidity of the situation hit me. I stopped him.

"Hold on. How is me giving you thirty euros going to solve anything? This is ridiculous. There is no risk. I have a European passport, I'm legally allowed to enter Europe and so is my motorcycle. This isn't legal."

"I can make big problems for you," he replied, suddenly angry. "You will have to wait here many days."

"I can make problems too," I said. "What happens when I report your request for a bribe?"

"There is nobody to report to. I am in charge here. This is the only way you will enter Europe."

I thought about my options. It was possible that he was bluffing and if I pushed the point he might cave, but he may not have been and I couldn't afford to be wrong. I wasn't allowed go back into Russia and he knew it.

"Fine." I reluctantly gave up. "I will give you fifteen euro."

He agreed, then checked the hallway for security cameras. "Go into the bathroom and put the money in your passport, then go and give it to the girl at the customs window."

"No," I replied. This was ridiculous. "I will give you the money in my passport and you will take it to her. You're the one that wants the bribe."

He agreed, the bribe was payed and I left in a huff.

I spent the next hour setting up camp outside a small village and trying to boil some water for dinner while being eaten by mosquitoes. They were swarming, more than I'd seen even in Siberia, a thick cloud of vampirous insects that were intent on draining every capillary in my body. I was forced to give up on food and seek refuge inside my tent, but they followed me before I could close the zipper.

I left the tent, walked thirty metres down the lane and waited. The mosquitoes only took a moment to catch up. I let them settle all over my arms then suddenly sprinted back to the tent and did the zipper up as fast as possible. I fell asleep listening to the high-pitched whine of the frustrated swarm.

—

I woke with the sun, skipped breakfast and saddled Noddy. Home was now a magnet, pulling stronger and stronger as each day brought me closer. Noddy seemed equally eager and raised no issues when we putted back out onto the road and turned south.

The sun swung from behind to sit on our left, flashing in golden bursts from behind the dark birch and pine forest that towered over the road.

I passed through a town called Daugavpils, a green, quiet place with trams trundling along tree-lined boulevards. I once again entertained the daydream of what life might be like if I just parked Noddy and lived here, but mostly my mind was empty - focused on the road, whether I was going to the right way, wondering when to fill the tank and simply absorbing the views, or the people and places that passed by as the surroundings changed from countryside to city and to countryside once again.

Not far past Daugavpils the road crossed a small bridge. A blue sign on the other side read 'Lietuvos Respublika'. Lithuania.

I decided to take a detour to see the capital, Vilnius,

which is only two hours from the border. I was able to leave Noddy next to a park in the city centre while I sipped a coffee at an open-air place nearby. The café had an old upright piano near the tables. A young guy sat and played. The slightly out-of-tune keys sent a clumsy melody out onto the street, turning the heads of suited men and women walking to work.

I sat and people-watched for a time, noting that a few people gave me second glances when they walked past. I looked down at my clothes. I was wearing the same brown leather jacket I'd bought in Ulaanbaatar, the same oil-and-grease stained jeans and the same Mongol-style horse riding boots buckled to my feet. My beard was large, unkempt and red, my hair was long and greasy. A massif of pimples had emerged where the helmet met my forehead. It wasn't, I realized, a subtle look.

After a few hours looking at the sights of central Vilnius I pressed on. The city gave way to some of the most scenic countryside I'd seen. Rutted dirt tracks weaved their way between small green hillocks, past lily-covered ponds and ancient wooden barns that hid in groves of oak and birch. Fields of yellow wheat flowed like gentle rivers between islands of deep green forest, dotted with small villages marked by lonely church steeples pointing at the warm blue sky. The ever-present noise of Noddy's engine seemed to fade away as I returned to the dance, leaning left, right, opening the throttle to surge out of the curves.

I crossed the Polish border that same afternoon (Lithuania is also tiny) and went to fill up at a petrol station. I went to pay and realized that the only words I'd said all day were "cappuccino, please" back in Vilnius.

"Uh, pump two," I said with a guttural rasp. I coughed and tried again, but my voice still sounded like a metal pipe being dragged over rough pavement.

I set up camp in a farmer's field several hundred metres from the road. This was a nervous night. I woke to the sound of every engine, wondering if it was the farmer and whether he'd inadvertently wrap me inside a hay bale.

———

I arrived in Warsaw the next morning and enjoyed another quiet coffee in the only café that seemed to be open. It was earlier than I realized. The ground isn't comfortable enough to spend much time sleeping on, so I was usually awake by six.

The woman running the café seemed startled at my appearance. I was probably extremely smelly and clearly my efforts to mask it with deodorant weren't working.

I walked to the centre of Warsaw and discovered a pleasant old city of markets set in cobbled squares, cathedrals and castle battlements. I stopped at a central square to take some photos. A woman wearing full black leathers pulled up next to Noddy on a motorcycle.

"Hi," I said, taking her by surprise as she removed her helmet.

"Uh, hello?"

"Do you mind taking a photo?" I held up my camera.

"Oh, sure, no problem."

She took the photo and handed back the camera. "This is your bike?" she asked, motioning towards Noddy.

"Yeah, that's mine. Where are you riding to?"

"I go to Greece," she replied. "Through Croatia, Macedonia, you know?"

I nodded. "That'll be nice. I haven't been, would love to. It'd be so good on a bike."

"And where do you ride from?"

"Uh, from Mongolia. But I got a lift from Novosibirsk to Moscow."

"From Mongolia? And you went across Mongolia?" She tucked a wayward lock of hair behind her ear.

"Yeah, over a few weeks. I'm enjoying being back on a road."

"I would love to do that," she said. "It's crazy, but I am a little crazy too. One day I will do the same."

"I recommend it! But maybe on a better motorcycle than this one."

She laughed. "Definitely. Anyway, it was nice to meet you."

"You too. Have a good time in Greece!"

It was becoming increasingly strange to think that I'd ridden here from Mongolia. Much later, long after the trip was over, I was browsing a hiker's guide in a bookstore and saw a quote (possibly by John Muir): "Our planet is made of many worlds, different from each other in almost every way, that intersect only momentarily." Warsaw certainly felt worlds away from the steppe, let alone from Guangzhou, from Bagan, from Perth. I could almost pinpoint the moments I'd moved from one world to another - disembarking the cruise ship in Singapore, arriving at the train station in Nanjing, crossing into Russia, waking up in a motel outside Moscow.

After a few hours in Warsaw I pushed on along a wide motorway towards the Czech Republic.

In the early afternoon I became hopelessly lost in Wroclaw but eventually found my way out and turned off the main highway to take smaller back-country roads across the border. The road passed across a flat land of yellow and green fields before rising into low foothills.

I stopped at a mechanic to borrow some tools and

change Noddy's oil, the last time I'd have to do so, then pressed on and soon passed a sign; "Česká republika."

Soon after the border the road plunged into dark, forested valleys, where it ran alongside a stream and through small villages of pubs and churches. Eventually, however, the road came to a dead end. The asphalt had been dug up. I turned back and followed a detour sign but soon got lost following the road through ever deeper gorges of big rivers lined by sheer, dark hills.

Eventually I came to the top of a hill and slept in a field, just by the edge of a deep, brooding forest. The Czech countryside stretched away before me as I heated a pot of noodles over a choppy sea of forested hills lying under summer's evening haze. I didn't know it at the time, but this was the last night I'd spend in the tent.

—

Noddy chucked his final tantrum the next morning. When I came to a traffic light in Prague I pushed the rear brake and nothing happened. I quickly pulled the front brake with a surge of adrenalin and came to a sudden stop. My heart sank and I pulled over as soon as possible.

I'll quickly explain what had gone wrong. Noddy's rear brake worked using a lever – when I pushed on the pedal with my foot, a horizontal rod pulled on a vertical lever which applied the brake. The single screw holding the horizontal rod to the vertical lever had vanished, so the whole mechanism was in pieces.

I sat on the curb, awash with a numbing sense of despair. I was only a thousand kilometres from Basel but I was stuck with a motorcycle without a rear brake, the one I needed most. Stopping with the front brake risked sending me flying over the handlebars. It was a Saturday, so I would probably have to wait until Monday to find a mechanic.

A man walked past and glanced at me sitting on the curb.

"Excuse me," I said, jumping to my feet. I pointed at the motorcycle. "Can you help? Do you know where I can find a mechanic?"

He looked around uncertainly. "No, no, sorry."

"Mechanic? Near here?"

"No, no." He walked quickly away.

I rubbed my face for a few seconds, then decided the best thing to do would be to ignore the problem completely. I rode into the centre of Prague and left Noddy on a road where there was a strong possibility he'd get towed. At least then he would no longer be my problem.

I tried a few hostels but they were all fully booked. Eventually I gave up and stayed in a hotel that was way above my budget. I was down to my last few hundred dollars, but I would be home soon and I certainly wasn't in the mood to get back on Noddy and find somewhere to set up camp. It was so worth it. I had a long, long shower, scrubbed off the dirt and grease and oil, and washed my hair and my beard.

I spent a day wandering around Prague's cobbled alleyways and past groups of tourists on Segways. The city was heaving. I was once again another backpacker wandering aimlessly in flip flops. After seeing the main sights I sat in a cafe and read my book for hours. My mind, as was becoming its habit, started to think of home.

—

The next morning I walked back to where I left Noddy. Unfortunately he was still sitting there when I turned the corner. He gave me a stupid look.

I stood next to him and thought through my options. I didn't have much in the way of tools. I did, however, still have that roll of duct tape I bought in Naran Tuul. I also had an empty bottle of Coke Zero that I'd finished the night before. An idea formed.

I took the bottle cap off, made a small hole in it with my pocketknife, then used most of the roll to tape it onto the horizontal rod where the screw used to be. I couldn't use the brake like I normally would, but hopefully this would knock a few kilometres off my speed if I needed to stamp on it in an emergency.

And so, with Noddy held together with a bottle cap and some duct tape, I set off. I soon crossed into Germany and took the autobahn south. I stayed in the hard shoulder while other vehicles roared by at well over twice my speed. Every so often a large truck or passenger van slowed down as it passed by and gave me a glimpse of a curious face pressed against the glass.

I sat on Noddy, holding the throttle open with my right hand and doing anything to occupy my mind as I sat alone inside my helmet. Noddy rattled and clunked along. The kilometres ticked by.

I did have a few interesting thoughts while I daydreamed the time away. For instance, all the energy we expel comes from the food we eat. That means we are our food's afterlife. Another interesting thought is that women are born with all of their egg cells. This means my first cell actually existed thirty years before I was born. How about that?

Once these thoughts ran out I began reading all the road signs to myself in a Scottish accent. I actually became so gripped by this new hobby that I missed the turnoff to Stuttgart by thirty-five kilometres, which was half an hour at Noddy's pace.

I arrived in Stuttgart in the late evening and found a room in an Ibis Budget. All the nearby restaurants were closed, so I bought a reheated sandwich from a petrol station and lay in bed in my underwear to read the end of The Lord of the Rings, when Sam returned home to the Shire; "Well, I'm back," he said.

—

I arrived at the Swiss border at lunchtime the next day and pulled over to ask the border guard where I should go to sort out Noddy's paperwork.

"Can you help me?" I called to him, taking my helmet off. "I bought this bike in Mongolia."

"What?".

"I bought this bike in Mongolia and would like to take it into Switzerland."

"Moldova?"

"No, Mongolia."

"You bought that in Mongolia?" he asked incredulously.

"Yes."

He laughed and yelled towards the guard monitoring the other lane of traffic.

"Hey, this guy bought this motorcycle in Mongolia!"

"WHAT?" the other guard shouted back.

"HE BOUGHT IT IN MONGOLIA!"

They both laughed and he turned back to me. "Go to that building," he pointed, chuckling. "Mongolia. Ha."

I followed his directions and was soon seated in front of two Swiss customs officials.

"So, you ride here from Mongolia," the woman asked. "How long does this take?"

"I got a lift across Russia, but altogether three weeks. Two weeks across Russia and almost one week from Moscow to here."

"This is… not usual." She looked at me with a curious smile. "Why did you do this?"

I shrugged. "It seemed like the best option at the time."

She laughed. "I have worked here a long, long time and I have never seen a Mongolian motorcycle."

She flipped through Noddy's paperwork. It was, of course, all in Mongolian.

"Do you know what is the chassis number?"

I leaned over the desk. "Uh, no, but maybe it is that one?" I pointed at a random sequence of numbers and letters.

"Maybe. We can use that one, it is ok."

They stamped me through and wished me good luck.

I returned to Noddy and took a quick photo. This was it, I thought. Even if I didn't get to Basel, I'd travelled from Australia to Switzerland without flying. The thought, oddly, came and went quickly, as if it were of no importance.

Then I rode off and soon saw a sign: Bern, 143 km, Basel 105 km.

Suddenly it hit me. I'd made it. From Sydney to Melbourne, across the Nullarbor, over the ocean to Singapore; with Max and Maisie in Malaysia, Ko Lanta, dinners in Bangkok, Sarah and Amy in Myanmar, the cave by the lake; to Laos, Luke, Spiderman and Mat and Hannah in Cambodia, the writhing trees in the ruins of Ta Prohm; north to China, Tim, and onwards to Mongolia, to Bata and Gantur; across the vast Mongol steppe, into the taiga forest with Magsar and Anka, over barren rocky plains and up into the Altai; through the enormous

Siberian birch forests with Sasha and Elena, over the Urals, across the countryside of Eastern Europe – all leading to here, on the sunny side of this Swiss motorway.

I rode into Zurich. I was staying on my friend Niki's couch and once I was nearby I pulled over near a tram stop and called her mobile. Noddy caught the eyes of many people walking past - casual glances that turned into stares before politeness pulled their eyes away. I scuffed my heels on the pavement and leaned against Noddy, finding comfort from his familiar shape.

Niki soon found me and I had a relaxing afternoon enjoying the small things, like brushing my teeth with a tap rather than a water bottle, eating home-cooked food and talking to someone I'd known a long time. We spend a while catching up in a café. Niki's tea came with a sand timer that told her exactly how long to leave the tea bag in. I'd come from Mongolia, where nothing is ever on time, to Switzerland, where even teabags aren't late.

—

I packed Noddy for the last time. Niki watched as I put my pack on the rack, the small bag on top of that, and tied it all together with my illegal Mongolian license plate facing backwards. The straps I was using had holes burnt into them by the exhaust pipe.

"What are you going to do with the bike once you get home?" Niki asked when I raised a leg over the seat and hopped into position.

I looked down and instinctively rested a hand on the gas tank.

"I'm not sure. There's not much on him that works. I

might keep him at my parents' until I figure something out. We'll see."

She laughed. "I still can't believe that's your motorcycle. Let alone that you brought it here from Mongolia."

"It is odd," I agreed. "It is a bit odd."

Noddy coughed to life and I pulled away, honking a shrill goodbye. After a few wrong turns I eventually found the motorway and began following the signs to Basel.

All of sudden, everything became familiar. The motorway ran past towns with names I knew, skirted farms and hills I'd seen before and entered tunnels I knew were coming.

Noddy was making more clunky metallic noises than ever and was now bleeding all over my jeans. The liquid was hot against my leg. I caught myself patting him affectionately, willing him onwards, as we merged into the growing traffic and disappeared.

EPILOGUE

It was surprisingly easy to come home. One of the most common questions I was asked was whether I was struggling to adjust, but that wasn't the case. It was odd, in some ways, that I'd chosen to stop at that particular point - some shallow forested valley in northern Switzerland. It seemed as if I was only going to be there for a few days before heading off again. Yet I was too busy enjoying the novelty of the small things – waking up in my own bed with nowhere to go, walking upstairs and seeing my parents, eating a regular breakfast – to dwell too much. Danika arrived in Basel a few days after I arrived. Those weeks were spent in the company of everyone I'd missed most while I was away. Life continued as it always had.

For the curious, I did manage to keep a record of every vehicle I used: 19 cars, 24 buses, 24 trains, six boats, four mopeds or motorcycles, two trams, fifteen vans and five tuk-tuks (99 vehicles in total). This number doesn't include the means of transport I used to explore areas, which mostly involved my own feet as well as innumerable tuk-tuks, mopeds, boats, bicycles and a few reindeer. Noddy and I travelled roughly 6000 kilometres together. The total distance I travelled, again not including local exploration, is (very roughly) 35,000 kilometres – not far off the circumference of the Earth.

As for the people I met – Herarn keeps in touch, Frank and Valda continue to cruise the world, Max and Maisie moved to Melbourne, Gantur bought a KTM motorcycle and began studying economics in Ulaanbaatar, Jimmy has gone on many more adventures and built a strong photography profile, and Sasha ended up getting that job with the World Wildlife Fund and has since gone from success to success. As far as I know, Magsar and his family remain in the forest. I intend to go back to

Mongolia and bring him some more steel wire.

Noddy and I parted ways unexpectedly. When I arrived in Basel I parked him and left in a car, then delayed retrieving him. There wasn't much I could do with Noddy. I'd have to recycle him because he was too old, weak and broken to ride or sell, but I had no way of legally getting him to the recycling plant. It was a difficult problem that was easy to ignore.

Eventually I returned to the car park to bring him home. I turned the corner to where I'd parked him, but he wasn't there. Puzzled, I searched the car park, walking past rows and rows of scooters and motorcycles thinking someone had moved him.

To this day I do not know what fate he came to. In all likelihood he was probably towed and scrapped. I, however, like to imagine that someone else found him and rode off towards Mongolia. Maybe he really is still out there, clunking and rattling along, leaving a line of mysterious liquid on the road behind while he whines towards some distant horizon.

As for me, my memories of this journey have faded with time. There are now some photos that I don't remember taking, people whose names I can no longer remember, events that I can no longer place in order. I'm sure, as time goes on, this gradual fading will continue.

Yet there are some memories that remain as clear today as they ever have. Every so often they surge forward and always at the most unexpected times – when I'm sitting at traffic lights, staring out a bus window, even in mid-conversation. It is almost as if I'm suddenly looking through someone else's eyes. For a few moments, the world disappears and I find myself shivering on the Great Wall, weaving Noddy through a barren valley, eating honeyberry jam in a cosy cottage, or sitting on a reindeer high above a vast, primal land, in the welcoming embrace of a cold wind.

About the Author

Ewen is a journalist and writer based in Australia. Overland is his first book.

Overland

Ingram Content Group UK Ltd.
Milton Keynes UK
UKHW040613240323
419098UK00002B/341